The Gospel According to Luke

Daniel J. Harrington, S.J.

William H. Sadlier, Inc.
New York   Chicago   Los Angeles

Nihil Obstat:
Rev. Matthew P. Stapleton
Censor Deputatus

Imprimatur:
✠ Humberto Cardinal Medeiros
Archdiocese of Boston
July 17,1982

Library of Congress Catalog Card Number: 82-061458
International Standard Book Number: 0-8215-5929-X
 23456789/987654

Published by
William H. Sadlier, Inc.
11 Park Place
New York, New York 10007

Printed and bound in the United States of America

The text of the Gospel of Luke and all other quotations from Scripture are from the *Good News Bible*, the Bible in Today's English Version. Copyright © American Bible Society, 1976.

Contents

"Easy access to sacred Scripture should be provided for all the Christian faithful."

Preface

The study of Scripture is among the oldest and most traditional religious activities in our Christian heritage. The Gospel of Mark and the Gospel of Luke begin their account of Jesus' public ministry by telling us that he read and preached on the Scriptures in the synagogue in Galilee. It was through their knowledge of the Scriptures that Jesus explained the meaning of his death and resurrection to the two disciples on the way to Emmaus. Readings from the Scriptures have been part of our liturgies since the time of the apostles.

Since the Scriptures are not contemporary works, today's audience needs some guidance to understand fully what the authors are trying to communicate to us about the faith of their communities and the events that generated that great faith. Like most carefully written and thoughtful literature, the books of the Bible have depths of meaning not always apparent to the casual reader. Experience tells us that clear guidance and attentive study can be the key to deeper understanding that will lead to rewarding reflection and prayer.

The *Access Guide* series is designed to help beginning and experienced readers of the sacred Scriptures arrive at a better understanding of the books of the

Bible and a familiarity with their role in the development of faith. Each book has been written by a noted authority on that particular part of the Bible. The language is clear, and the text presented in a highly readable manner.

The general introduction of each study guide acquaints the reader with the background of the particular book of the Bible being studied. It provides information about the biblical author, the historical period in which the book was written, and the nature of the community that was the first audience for the book. The theological themes which summarize the author's message are also discussed, giving the reader an idea of what to look for in considering each section of the book.

A thumbnail sketch of each book of the Bible provides the reader with a basic outline that indicates how the author organized his account of the events in order better to communicate his message. It is interesting to note that, in their original form, the books of the Bible were not divided into chapters and verses. Most had no punctuation or even spaces between the words. The organization of the text, as we know it today, took place at a much later date. Often this organization was done by scholars who failed to appreciate the original organization of the authors' thoughts. The sections of the books are organized in these guides in such a way as to reflect the natural internal flow of the original authors' manuscripts.

Likewise, since the ancient Hebrew, Greek, and Aramaic languages are no longer commonly spoken, there are many variations in the way the Scriptures are translated into English. The preferred translation for this series is the *Good News Bible* because of its readability in contemporary English. The reader may choose another translation or wish to compare translations which vary. Certainly, recognizing differences in the interpretation of the Scriptures will enhance the reader's ability to get more out of each passage.

The *Access Guide* series is designed for both group and individual study. All the information needed to use the study guides is provided. Groups, however, may wish to have a discussion leader and use the edition of the *Access Guide* which contains notes for the discussion leader. It is also encouraged that individual readers and groups participants have a complete Bible on hand for reference purposes.

The material in each study guide is arranged into six study sessions. This format will help those in discussion groups plan each session around a specific sequence of the Scripture text and give some direction to the discussions. A group leader may find it more convenient to rearrange the material into a greater or fewer number of sessions.

Each of the six study sessions contains a portion of Scripture and commentary. Questions for discussion and reflection are meant to lead the reader to probe more deeply into the significance of the Scripture for its first audience and for the contemporary Christian. Naturally, a renewed understanding of the Scriptures and a fresh discovery of the riches contained therein will lead to reflection and prayer and be shared with others through discussion and celebration.

General Introduction to Luke, Gospel to the Gentiles

The Place of Luke in the New Testament and in the Church

Luke intended his life of Jesus and his story of the early Church, the Acts of the Apostles, to be read together. In this respect he differs from the other evangelists who ended their stories with the resurrection of Jesus and his appearances to the disciples. The artistry and literary grace of Luke's Gospel have won it the description as "the most beautiful book ever written." That accolade rests in part on its stirring hymns, memorable parables, contrasting characters, and marvelous portrait of Jesus as prophet and example.

The earliest ascription of this Gospel to Luke, the companion of Paul, comes from the late second century. The so-called Muratorian Fragment claims that Luke was Paul's companion as "an expert in the way" and that, because he was not an eyewitness to Jesus, he had to rely on sources for his Gospel. From the references to the companion of Paul who was named Luke (Philemon 24; Colossians 4:14; and 2 Timothy 4:11), he appears to have been a physician and a gentile. Moreover, the famous "we" passages in Acts suggest that the author of Acts accompanied Paul on his sea voyages.

The debate about the relationship between the author of Luke-Acts and Paul's companion named Luke is very complicated and has much more relevance for interpreting Acts than it does for the Gospel. But whatever judgment is made about the historical relationship between Luke and Paul, it is important not to read Luke's Gospel through the spectacles of Pauline theology. There certainly are affinities between Luke's theology and Paul's theology. Both emphasize the universal offer of salvation, Jesus as Lord, God's love for sinners, the importance of faith, and so on. But the important differences between them must not be ignored. For example, whereas Paul emphasized the atoning or sacrificial value of Jesus' death, Luke was more concerned with its exemplary character in giving us a model of how to relate to God and to our enemies. Even if Luke the evangelist was Paul's companion, he clearly developed an independent vision of the elements of Christian faith. Luke deserves to be recognized as a perceptive and creative theological thinker in his own right.

Luke was able to express his theological vision with great artistic skill. The literary beauty of his Gospel and its compelling portrait of Jesus have won for it a central place in the devotional life of the Church. During the Christmas season Luke 1:5—2:52 is especially prominent in the official worship of the Church and in the consciousness of the general public. Phrases from the other parts of the Gospel such as "good Samaritan," "prodigal son," and "good thief" are part of everyday English speech.

The Gospel of Luke has a particular relevance for Christians in the late twentieth century. In a world that searches without much success for models of goodness and integrity, Jesus' fidelity to his Father and to his own teachings stands out sharply and brightly. For a Church that runs the risk of being pushed to the sidelines of society and being declared useless, Luke's stress on the place of Jesus and the Church in world history is a timely reminder to resist this marginalization.

The Gospel's special concern for the outsiders of society challenges our Church to share its spiritual and material treasures with the economically and culturally poor, with the sick and the despised, the people at the lowest levels of society, with all the outsiders in our world. At a point in history when the gap between the rich and the poor seems to be growing larger than ever, Luke impresses on the rich that it is their religious duty to share their good things with the poor. For all those in pursuit of a deeper and more genuine spirituality, Luke shows us when and how to pray. All those who might be overwhelmed by the needs of people in our world and by the apparent inability of the Church and society in general to meet these needs are reminded that God guides history according to his plan and that we are at best instruments of his Holy Spirit.

The Purpose of the Writer and the Nature of the Community

In his preface to the Gospel, Luke tells us what he was trying to do and why. He wished to provide an orderly account of the "things that have taken place among us." These things were the life, death, and resurrection of Jesus, as well as the spread of the Christian mission from Jerusalem to Rome. Luke freely admitted that many others had already taken up this task, and that he himself was not an eyewitness to the events described in the Gospel. Even though Luke was modest in his claims ("I thought it would be good . . ."), he was very serious about achieving his goal: that his readers might know the truth about Jesus Christ and the earliest days of the Church.

Luke's own statement of purpose indicates that he set out to write a *didactic biography*. Greek and Latin writers of Luke's time wrote biographies about emperors, generals, and other famous figures. They stated their methods and goals in much the same way that Luke talked about his project in 1:1–4. These biographers were more interested in the hero's moral or religious significance than in writing a historically accurate account of the events in his life. The subject of the biography was presented as an example either to be imitated or to be avoided. His life had teaching or *didactic* value. So Luke sought to tell the story of Jesus in a literary form that would have been familiar to educated people in the Mediterranean world of the first century A.D.

Both the Gospel and Acts are dedicated to someone named Theophilus. The name means "lover of God." It is hard to know whether this Theophilus was Luke's literary patron, a powerful person whom Luke wished to win over to Christianity, a Christian friend, or a symbolic name for all lovers of God who will find enjoyment and instruction in the story of Jesus and the early Church. Luke surely intended his two-volume work for a wider audience. He seems specifically to have had in mind Christians who were not Jewish by birth, but who were acquainted with the Old Testament and Jewish life. Those gentiles who were attracted to Judaism's teachings about God and its high ethical standards were called "God-fearers." Luke himself may have been a God-fearer, and the community for which he wrote probably included many such people.

Since Acts ends before Paul's death, it has been frequently asserted that Luke-Acts was composed in the 60s of the first century A.D. Luke, however, appears to have used Mark's Gospel as a source, and that Gospel was composed around A.D. 70. Furthermore, the language of Jesus' "predictions" about the destruction of Jerusalem in Luke 19:43—44 and 21:20—24 seems to assume a knowledge of events that had already taken place. Therefore the composition of Luke-Acts is usually dated around A.D. 80—90.

The place of composition is uncertain. It has been assigned to Rome, Greece, Asia Minor (present-day Turkey), Syria, and Palestine. Recent scholarship seems to favor two locations, Antioch in Syria and Caesarea on the coast of Palestine, but there is no certainty on this matter.

Literary Patterns

Luke's most obvious achievement was the order or outline that he placed on his sources. He used the Gospel of Mark in three large blocks:

Luke 3:1—6:19   Mark 1:1—3:19
Luke 8:4—9:50   Mark 3:20—6:44; 8:27—9:50
Luke 18:15—24:12   Mark 10:1—16:8

The large section of Mark's Gospel not used by Luke (Mark 6:45—8:26) is sometimes called Luke's "great omission." Perhaps the copy of Mark that was available to Luke lacked this material.

It is fair to call the Gospel of Luke a revision or a second edition of Mark's Gospel. Luke apparently set out to improve Mark's Greek by avoiding foreign words, omitting colloquial expressions, and giving the story of Jesus a more elevated style. As a careful editor, Luke wanted to set aside some possibly offensive points and to clear up misunderstandings and obscurities. But most of all, Luke wished to include source material that was not available to Mark, and so to provide a fuller and richer portrait of Jesus.

Like Matthew, Luke apparently had access to the collection of Jesus' sayings that is usually designated by the letter Q (from the German *Quelle,* meaning "source"). He used most of this material in the two blocks that fall between the Markan blocks. The first of these non-Markan blocks (6:20—8:3) is sometimes called "the small insertion," and the second (9:51—18:14) is called the "large insertion." These two sections also include many traditions found only in Luke.

The basic geographical and theological outline that Luke imposed on these sources follows this pattern:

the preparation (1:5—4:13)
the public ministry in Galilee (4:14—9:50)
the journey up to Jerusalem (9:51—19:44)
the ministry in the Temple at Jerusalem (19:45—21:38)
the death and resurrection in Jerusalem (22:1—24:53)

The most striking feature in this outline is the large amount of space devoted to the journey of Jesus and his disciples up to Jerusalem in 9:51—19:44. Along the way Jesus instructs his followers about himself and about the path of discipleship.

In addition to presenting the story of Jesus, Luke has included some of the most memorable literary pieces in the New Testament. The hymns sung by Mary, Zechariah, and Simeon have influenced the language of worship for 2,000 years. The parables of the good Samaritan, the prodigal son, and the rich man and Lazarus are masterful examples of storytelling. The sharp contrasts between characters like the unjust judge and the persistent widow or between the Pharisee and the tax collector at prayer are exquisitely drawn.

The characters in the Gospel are presented as models or examples. In the infancy stories of chapters 1–2 Zechariah and Elizabeth, Mary, and Simeon and Anna represent the best features in Israel's tradition of faith. But the most important example is Jesus himself. Proclaimed in public as the Son of God at his baptism, Jesus sets the pattern for his disciples and for all Christians in his teachings and healing activity. Even in his death on the cross, he forgives his enemies and entrusts himself totally to his heavenly Father.

Major Theological Themes

Even a casual reading of Luke's Gospel reveals how dependent the evangelist was on early Christian traditions for his portrait of Jesus. He insists on the decisive importance of Jesus' death and resurrection. He takes over the titles son of David, Messiah or Christ, Son of Man, Son of God, and Lord. Perhaps the most distinctive feature in Luke's presentation is his emphasis on Jesus as a prophet. Jesus was foreshadowed by the prophets of the Old Testament and brings to fulfillment the entire prophetic tradition. Like the prophets of old, Jesus is rejected and put to death in Jerusalem, an event that makes possible the birth of the prophetic community of the Church. That death was a divine necessity foretold by the prophets. The innocent Jesus dies a martyr's death. He is faithful to his own teachings until the very end.

Luke deliberately situates the story of Jesus in the context of world history. He gives the dates of the various rulers and traces the spread of the movement begun by Jesus from Jerusalem to Rome in Acts. Every effort is made to show that Jesus was innocent of any political crime and that the Roman empire had nothing to fear from him and the early Christians.

Jesus' words and deeds express God's special love for the "outsiders" of society. Among the outsiders are the people of the infancy story, Zechariah and Elizabeth, Mary, the shepherds, and Simeon and Anna. During his public ministry, Jesus heals lepers, people possessed by demons, and the sick and handicapped. He preaches the good news of God's kingdom to tax collectors and sinners, women, and the poor. He presents Samaritans in positive ways, and points toward the gentiles as worthy objects of God's concern. Even during his suffering on the cross, he holds out to a criminal the promise of life in heaven.

The relationship between the rich and the poor of society was one of Luke's special concerns. Perhaps his own community included both rich and poor members. Through the traditions about Jesus, Luke warned the rich that material wealth is not the most important thing in life and that the rich have a serious obligation to share their wealth with the poor. He also encouraged the poor to respond to Jesus' invitation to God's kingdom and to recognize that one's standing before God is far more significant than one's place in human society.

Luke's Gospel is often called the Gospel of prayer, because it presents Jesus as praying at the key points in his life and because it includes several instructions on prayer not found in the other Gospels. Jesus prays at his baptism, in response to the crowd's enthusiasm over his miracles, before choosing the twelve apostles, before Peter identifies him as the Messiah, prior to the transfiguration, after the Last Supper and before his arrest, and at the moment of his death. At each point, Jesus' prayer expresses his unique relationship with his heavenly Father. When asked by his disciples for a sample prayer, Jesus teaches them to address God as Father and to bring their needs to him. He encourages a surprising persistence in prayer, since God wishes to hear our prayers and to answer them.

The Holy Spirit is a major figure in the early parts of the Gospel. Jesus is conceived by the Holy Spirit, and people like Zechariah and Simeon prophesy about Jesus through the inspiration of the Holy Spirit. Just as the Holy Spirit came upon Jesus at baptism, the Spirit of the Lord is upon him at the very beginning of his public ministry. That Jesus is the sole agent of the Holy Spirit throughout his ministry is made clear in the healings and other powerful actions. After his ascension, Jesus promises to pour out the Holy Spirit on the disciples. In other words, the Holy Spirit is the principle of continuity between the time of the Old Testament, the time of Jesus, and the time of the Church. In the Acts of the Apostles, the Holy Spirit is active in the Church and is responsible for its growth. Luke makes it clear that conversion, the gift of the Spirit, and baptism go together.

A Thumbnail Sketch of Luke

In his Gospel, Luke set out to give a connected account of the life, death, and resurrection of Jesus. He did this in order to bolster his readers' confidence in the truth of the Christian message. As we have seen in the preceding chapter, Luke imposed on the early Christian sources available to him a geographical plan.

The stories about the births of John the Baptist and Jesus (1:5—2:52) move between Judea (Jerusalem and its environs) and Galilee (Nazareth). After the period of preparation around the Jordan River (3:1—4:13), Jesus begins his public ministry in Galilee (4:14–30). The first phase of it consists of preaching and healing.

The second and central phase of Jesus' public ministry (9:51—19:44) takes the form of a journey that starts with rejection in a Samaritan village, returns to Galilee, and reaches its end with the entrance into the Temple in Jerusalem. This journey is the vehicle for Luke to include many teachings about who Jesus is (Christology) and who his followers are in relation to him (discipleship). The Jerusalem Temple is the base of operation for the third phase of Jesus' public ministry (19:45—21:38). There he teaches daily and outwits those who seek to trap him.

The story of the passion, death, and resurrection of Jesus (22:1—24:53) occurs entirely in Jerusalem. In locating the passion and death in Jerusalem (22:1—24:12), Luke agrees with Matthew and Mark. But in placing the appearances of the risen Lord in and around Jerusalem (24:13—53), he differs from the other synoptic evangelists. Matthew and Mark situate the appearances in Galilee. Just as Luke's story of Jesus began in the Jerusalem Temple (1:9), so it ends there also (24:53).

An outline of the Gospel would look something like this:

Part One: **The Consolation of Israel (1:1—2:52)**
The prologue (1:1–4); the announcements of the births of John and Jesus (1:5–38); Mary's visit to Elizabeth (1:39–56); the birth and naming of John (1:57–80); the birth of Jesus (2:1–20); the circumcision and presentation of Jesus (2:21–40); Jesus in the Temple (2:41–52).

Part Two: **Son of God and Prophet (3:1—4:30)**
John's preparation (3:1–20); Jesus as Son of God in the baptism (3:21–22); the genealogy 3:23–28); and the testing (4:1–13); the beginning of Jesus' prophetic ministry in Galilee (4:14–30).

Part Three: **Powerful in Word and Deed (4:31—6:19)**
Teaching and healing (4:31–44); the call of the disciples (5:1–11); another healing and five conflicts (5:12–6:11); the choice of the twelve apostles and the scene of Jesus' teaching (6:12–19).

Part Four: **Teacher and Healer (6:20—8:3)**
The Sermon on the Plain (6:20–49); the healings of the centurion's servant (7:1–10) and the widow's son (7:11–17); Jesus and John (7:18–35); the sinful woman (7:36–50); the women disciples (8:1–3).

Part Five: **Revelation and Misunderstanding (8:4—9:50)**
Parables and explanations (8:4–21); miracles (8:22–56); the mission of the twelve apostles and the miraculous feeding (9:1–17); revelations and misunderstandings (9:18–50).

Part Six: **The Journey Begins (9:51—11:13)**
Rejection and discipleship (9:51–62); the mission of the seventy disciples (10:1–24); love of God and neighbor (10:25–11:13).

Part Seven: **The Journey Continues (11:14—13:30)**
The source of Jesus' power (11:14–36); true and false spiritualities (11:37–52); fearless confession (12:1–12); material concerns (12:13–34); watchfulness (12:35–48); admission to God's kingdom (12:49–13:30).

Part Eight: **The Journey Proceeds (13:31—16:31)**
Departure from Galilee (13:31–35); banquet teachings (14:1–35); parables of the lost (15:1–32); teachings about wealth (16:1–31).

Part Nine: **The Journey Ends (17:1—21:38)**
The disciples' responsibilities (17:1–19); the coming kingdom (17:20–37); prayer (18:1–14); entering the kingdom (18:15–19:27); arrival in Jerusalem (19:28–44); teachings at the Temple (19:45–21:4); the discourse on the end of the world (21:5–38).

Part Ten: **Martyr and Example (22:1—24:53)**
The Last Supper (22:1–38); Jesus' prayer and arrest (22:39–65); the trials (22:66–23:16); the sentencing and death (23:17–56); the empty tomb (24:1–12); the appearances of the risen Lord (24:13–53).

The Consolation of Israel ———— Luke 1:1—2:52

Unlike the other Gospel writers, Luke begins his Gospel with a clear statement of purpose (1:1—4). This statement contains the elements present in the prefaces to the biographies of other famous figures in ancient times: the dedication (to Theophilus), a description of the subject matter, a reference to previous writers, an expression of modesty ("I thought it would be good . . ."), and a claim to accuracy.

The description of the account as "orderly" in 1:3 does not necessarily refer to the chronological sequence of events. It could refer to the order that best contributes to expressing the significance of Jesus for the members of the community.

The Birth of John Announced

The central character in the story of the announcement of John's birth is Zechariah, the father of John. In 1:5—7 Luke provides us with some personal information: Zechariah lived in the time when Herod the Great ruled in Judea (37—4 B.C.), and he belonged to a priestly family, as did his wife Elizabeth. Members of the priestly families took turns in performing the rites at the Temple in Jerusalem, and so we are supposed to imagine Zechariah offering incense in the innermost part of the Temple.

Thus the story of our salvation begins in the Temple at Jerusalem. As it does in so many occasions in Luke's gospel, prayer plays an important part in this event. The moment is marked by the prayer of Zechariah the priest representing the united prayer of the devout community outside the sanctuary.

There are several points in the angel's description of the child to be born that link John with Samson (Judges 13) and with the prophet Elijah (Malachi 3:1; 4:5). For Luke, John the Baptizer is clearly identified as an Old Testament figure, introducing the presence of the Messiah and the kingdom.

The first episode in Luke introduces some themes that we will meet often in the Gospel: Jerusalem and the Temple there as the privileged place in the geography of our salvation, prayer as the appropriate activity at decisive moments, the joy and gladness that accompany the story of our salvation, and the Holy Spirit as directing that story.

The Gospel According to Luke

Introduction

1 Dear Theophilus:
Many have done their best to write a report of the things that have taken place among us. ²They wrote what we have been told by those who saw these things from the beginning and proclaimed the message. ³And so, your Excellency, because I have carefully studied all

these matters from their beginning, I thought it good to write an orderly account for you. ⁴I do this so that you will know the full truth of all those matters which you have been taught.

The Birth of John the Baptist Is Announced

⁵During the time when Herod was king of Judea, there was a priest named Zechariah, who belonged to the priestly order of Abiah. His wife's name was Elizabeth; she also belonged to a priestly family. ⁶They both lived good lives in God's sight, and obeyed fully all the Lord's commandments and rules. ⁷They had no children because Elizabeth could not have any, and she and Zechariah were both very old.

⁸One day Zechariah was doing his work as a priest before God, taking his turn in the daily service. ⁹According to the custom followed by the priests, he was chosen by lot to burn the incense on the altar. So he went into the Temple of the Lord, ¹⁰while the crowd of people outside prayed during the hour of burning the incense. ¹¹An angel of the Lord appeared to him, standing at the right side of the altar where the incense was burned. ¹²When Zechariah saw him he was troubled and felt afraid. ¹³But the angel said to him: "Don't be afraid, Zechariah! God has heard your prayer, and your wife Elizabeth will bear you a son. You are to name him John. ¹⁴How glad and happy you will be, and how happy many others will be when he is born! ¹⁵For he will be a great man in the Lord's sight. He must not drink any wine or strong drink. From his very birth he will be filled with the Holy Spirit. ¹⁶He will bring back many of the

people of Israel to the Lord their God. [17]He will go as God's messenger, strong and mighty like the prophet Elijah. He will bring fathers and children together again; he will turn the disobedient people back to the way of thinking of the righteous; he will get the Lord's people ready for him."

[18]Zechariah said to the angel, "How shall I know if this is so? I am an old man and my wife also is old." [19]"I am Gabriel," the angel answered. "I stand in the presence of God, who sent me to speak to you and tell you this good news. [20]But you have not believed my message, which will come true at the right time. Because you have not believed you will be unable to speak, you will remain silent until the day my promise to you comes true."

[21]In the meantime the people were waiting for Zechariah, wondering why he was spending such a long time in the Temple. [22]When he came out he could not speak to them—and so they knew that he had seen a vision in the Temple. Unable to say a word, he made signs to them with his hands.

[23]When his period of service in the Temple was over, Zechariah went back home. [24]Some time later his wife Elizabeth became pregnant, and did not leave the house for five months. [25]"Now at last the Lord has helped me in this way," she said. "He has taken away my public disgrace!"

Jesus' Birth Announced

The announcement of Jesus' birth follows the same outline as the announcement of John's birth: an encounter with the angel (1:26–27); a word of greeting (1:28–30); the commission to be Jesus' mother

(1:31–33); an objection by Mary (1:34); a reassurance (1:35); and a sign (1:36).

The announcements of the births of John and Jesus have many points in common: an obstacle to pregnancy; the appearance of the angel Gabriel; the birth announced beforehand; the naming before birth; the predictions of future greatness; the activity of the Holy Spirit; and the decisive place in the story of salvation.

In the accounts of the predictions of John's and Jesus' births one can also find a statement about the relation between John and Jesus. The titles applied to John and Jesus clearly indicate that Jesus is the greater, the one to whom John will give witness.

The Birth of Jesus Is Announced

[26]In the sixth month of Elizabeth's pregnancy God sent the angel Gabriel to a town in Galilee named Nazareth. [27]He had a message for a girl promised in marriage to a man named Joseph, who was a descendant of King David. The girl's name was Mary. [28]The angel came to her and said, "Peace be with you! The Lord is with you, and has greatly blessed you!" [29]Mary was deeply troubled by the angel's message, and she wondered what his words meant. [30]The angel said to her: "Don't be afraid, Mary, for God has been gracious to you. [31]You will become pregnant and give birth to a son, and you will name him Jesus. [32]He will be great and will be called the Son of the Most High God. The Lord God will make him a king, as his ancestor David was, [33]and he will be the king of the descendants of Jacob for ever; his kingdom will never end!"

³⁴Mary said to the angel, "I am a virgin. How, then, can this be?" ³⁵The angel answered: "The Holy Spirit will come on you, and God's power will rest upon you. For this reason the holy child will be called the Son of God. ³⁶Remember your relative Elizabeth. It is said that she cannot have children; but she herself is now six months pregnant, even though she is very old. ³⁷For there is not a thing that God cannot do."

³⁸"I am the Lord's servant," said Mary; "may it happen to me as you have said." And the angel left her.

The Visitation

The story of Mary's visit to Elizabeth consists of the event and a blessing. In the ancient Near East it was customary to praise parents on account of their remarkable children. In 1:42–45 Mary is blessed because of the child, Jesus, in her womb. Also, in ancient Israel the king's mother played a more prominent role than the king's wife, and so Mary is greeted as "my Lord's mother." Mary's response to Elizabeth's blessing (1:46–55) takes the form of a hymn full of phrases from the Old Testament. Mary praises God because God has exalted her (a lowly woman) so that all generations will call her blessed. Her case is an example of the way that God puts down the proud and raises up the lowly, and deals with Israel as his own special people. The birth of the child Jesus to an apparently insignificant woman in an unimportant country of the Roman empire will bring about a dramatic reversal of social relations and the fulfillment of God's promises to Israel. The hymn uses the Old Testament poetic device of parallelism: the same point is made twice, in either similar ways (1:51) or opposite ways (1:52–53).

In Mary's hymn we can see an identification between Mary and God's people. The history of salvation is filled with examples of God's choosing of the "lowly" to perform great deeds in the carrying out of God's will for his people. As Luke's story unfolds, Mary will be seen as a model for all believers, the first among the disciples of Jesus.

■ *Reflection*
For what events in my life have I found reason to praise God?

Mary Visits Elizabeth

[39]Soon afterward Mary got ready and hurried off to the hill country, to a town in Judea. [40]She went into Zechariah's house and greeted Elizabeth. [41]When Elizabeth heard Mary's greeting, the baby moved within her. Elizabeth was filled with the Holy Spirit, [42]and spoke in a loud voice: "Blessed are you among women! Blessed is the child you will bear! [43]Why should this great thing happen to me, that my Lord's mother comes to visit me? [44]For as soon as I heard your greeting, the baby within me jumped with gladness. [45]How happy are you to believe that the Lord's message to you will come true!"

Mary's Song of Praise

[46]Mary said:
"My heart praises the Lord,
[47]My soul is glad because of God my Savior.
[48]For he has remembered me, his lowly servant!

And from now on all people will call me
blessed,
⁴⁹Because of the great things the Mighty
God has done for me.
His name is holy;
⁵⁰He shows mercy to all who fear him,
From one generation to another.
⁵¹He stretched out his mighty arm
And scattered the proud people with all
their plans.
⁵²He brought down mighty kings from
their thrones,
And lifted up the lowly.
⁵³He filled the hungry with good things,
And sent the rich away with empty
hands.
⁵⁴He kept the promise he made to our
ancestors;
He came to the help of his servant
Israel,
⁵⁵And remembered to show mercy to
Abraham
And to all his descendants for ever!''

⁵⁶Mary stayed about three months with
Elizabeth, and then went back home.

John Is Born

After Mary returned home from her three month
stay, Elizabeth gave birth to a son and named him
John. In answer to the question about what this child
will be (1:66), Zechariah praises God with a hymn full of
Old Testament phrases. There are three major characters, God, the people, and the child John, and three
major themes, divine intervention, salvation, and the
prophetic word. In the hymn or prophesy of Zechariah
there is affirmation of John's relationship to Jesus. John
is the prophet who goes before, to prepare the way.

Jesus is called Lord—the salvation from the house of David. Disciples of John are called upon to join Zechariah in praising God for salvation brought through Jesus, announced by John.

The Birth of John the Baptist

⁵⁷The time came for Elizabeth to have her baby, and she gave birth to a son. ⁵⁸Her neighbors and relatives heard how wonderfully good the Lord had been to her, and they all rejoiced with her.

⁵⁹When the baby was a week old they came to circumcise him; they were going to name him Zechariah, his father's name. ⁶⁰But his mother said, "No! His name will be John." ⁶¹They said to her, "But you don't have a single relative with that name!" ⁶²Then they made signs to his father, asking him what name he would like the boy to have. ⁶³Zechariah asked for a writing pad and wrote, "His name is John." How surprised they all were! ⁶⁴At that moment Zechariah was able to speak again, and he started praising God. ⁶⁵The neighbors were all filled with fear, and the news about these things spread through all the hill country of Judea. ⁶⁶All who heard of it thought about it and asked, "What is this child going to be?" For it was plain that the Lord's power was with him.

⁶⁷His father Zechariah was filled with the Holy Spirit, and he prophesied:

> ⁶⁸"Let us praise the Lord, the God of Israel!
> For he came to the help of his people
> and set them free.
> ⁶⁹He raised up a mighty Savior for us,

One who is a descendant of his servant
David.
70 This is what he said long ago by means
of his holy prophets;
71 He promised to save us from our
enemies,
And from the power of all those who
hate us.
72 He said he would show mercy to our
ancestors,
And remember his sacred covenant.
73-74 He made a solemn promise to our ancestor Abraham,
And vowed that he would rescue us
from our enemies,
And allow us to serve him without fear,
75 To be holy and righteous before him,
All the days of our life.
76 You, my child, will be called a prophet
of the Most High God;
You will go ahead of the Lord
To prepare his road for him,
77 To tell his people that they will be
saved,
By having their sins forgiven.
78 For our God is merciful and tender;
He will cause the bright dawn of salvation to rise on us,
79 And shine from heaven on all those
who live in the dark shadow of
death,
To guide our steps into the path of
peace.''

80 The child grew and developed in body and
spirit; he lived in the desert until the day when
he would appear publicly to the people of
Israel.

Jesus Is Born

Luke sets the scene for Jesus' birth in 2:1–5. Ceasar Augustus was the Roman emperor from 27 B.C. to A.D. 14. According to Luke, Jesus was born before the death of Herod the Great in 4 B.C. The census was probably carried out on the local level from time to time, not all over the world at once. The return to the ancestral home for the census is paralleled in other ancient censuses. Since engaged couples did not customarily make such journeys together, we are to assume that Mary and Joseph had been married. Bethlehem is about eight miles south of Jerusalem. It was the home of King David about a thousand years before Christ.

The birth of Jesus most likely took place in one of the many caves in the hills surrounding Bethlehem that provided warmth and shelter for shepherds and their flocks. The new-born child was wrapped in cloths or strips of cloth, and placed in a box or trough from which the animals were fed.

Aside from references to Old Testament descriptions (Isaiah 1:3, Jeremiah 14:8), the circumstances of Jesus' birth related by Luke indicate his identification with the poor and the outcast. Here the descendant of David is an outsider in his own town.

Angels proclaim Jesus' birth to shepherds in the fields around Bethlehem. Shepherds had a low social status and were often suspected of dishonesty. Yet it is to shepherds that the joyous news of the savior's birth is first proclaimed. It is to such as these that Jesus came and preached and healed.

The story of Jesus' birth closes with the reactions of various people in 2:15–20. The shepherds respond to the angels' proclamation immediately. They go and find Mary, Joseph, and Jesus, and then tell about what happened to them. Luke tells us that all who heard the story were amazed at these happenings.

Just as John had been circumcised and named eight days after his birth (1:59), so Jesus was circumcised and named (2:21). Circumcision was understood as the sign of the relationship existing between God and his people.

The Birth of Jesus
(Also Matt. 1:18—25)

2 At that time Emperor Augustus sent out an order for all the citizens of the Empire to register themselves for the census. [2]When this first census took place, Quirinius was the governor of Syria. [3]Everyone then went to register himself, each to his own town.

[4]Joseph went from the town of Nazareth, in Galilee, to Judea, to the town named Bethlehem, where King David was born. Joseph went there because he himself was a descendant of David. [5]He went to register himself with Mary, who was promised in marriage to him. She was pregnant, [6]and while they were in Bethlehem, the time came for her to have her baby. [7]She gave birth to her first son, wrapped him in cloths and laid him in a manger—there was no room for them to stay in the inn.

The Shepherds and the Angels

[8]There were some shepherds in that part of the country who were spending the night in the fields, taking care of their flocks. [9]An angel of the Lord appeared to them, and the glory of the Lord shone over them. They were terribly afraid, [10]but the angel said to them: "Don't be

afraid! For I am here with goods news for you, which will bring great joy to all the people. [11]This very night in David's town your Savior was born—Christ the Lord! [12]This is what will prove it to you: you will find a baby wrapped in cloths and lying in a manger."

[13]Suddenly a great army of heaven's angels appeared with the angel, singing praises to God:

> [14]"Glory to God in the highest heaven!
> And peace on earth to men with whom
> he is pleased!"

[15]When the angels went away from them back into heaven, the shepherds said to one another, "Let us go to Bethlehem and see this thing that has happened, that the Lord has told us." [16]So they hurried off and found Mary and Joseph, and saw the baby lying in the manger. [17]When the shepherds saw him they told them what the angel had said about this child. [18]All who heard it were filled with wonder at what the shepherds told them. [19]Mary remembered all these things, and thought deeply about them. [20]The shepherds went back, singing praises to God for all they had heard and seen; it had been just as the angel had told them.

[21]A week later, when the time came for the baby to be circumcised, he was named Jesus—the name which the angel had given him before he had been conceived.

Temple Rites and Prophecies

The two rituals in 2:22–24 provide the occasion for bringing Jesus to the Temple in Jerusalem. According to Exodus 13, the first-born son is to be brought to the Temple. This rite is called the presentation. According to Leviticus 12, a woman who had given birth to a male child was not allowed in the Temple for forty days and until she brought an offering. This rite is called the purification.

The witness of Simeon to Jesus (2:25–35) takes place at the Temple in Jerusalem. Simeon's hymn in 2:29–32 uses phrases from the book of Isaiah (see 40:5; 52:10; 49:6; 42:6; 46:13), and explains what the consolation of Israel means. It seems clear that Simeon sees Jesus as the salvation of all the people of all the nations. The Messiah is to come through Israel to all the world.

Yet Simeon's words to Mary (2:34–35) prophesy opposition to Jesus. He will be a controversial figure for Israel, a "sign" from God which many people will speak against.

Another witness to Jesus in the Temple is Anna (2:36–38). As Simeon recognized Jesus to be the consolation of Israel, so Anna recognizes him as the redemption of Jerusalem. Anna and Simeon represent for Luke the faithful Israelites in contrast to the high priests and political leaders. They are favored by God because of their dedication and prayer. After the witness by Simeon and Anna, Jesus returns to Nazareth in Galilee.

■ Reflection
Does devotion to Mary play an important role in my spiritual life? How is it expressed?

Jesus Is Presented in the Temple

[22]The time came for Joseph and Mary to do what the Law of Moses commanded and perform the ceremony of purification. So they took the child to Jerusalem to present him to the Lord. [23]This is what is written in the law of the Lord: "Every first-born male shall be dedicated

to the Lord." ²⁴They also went to offer a sacrifice as required by the law of the Lord: "A pair of doves or two young pigeons."

²⁵Now there was a man living in Jerusalem whose name was Simeon. He was a good and God-fearing man and was waiting for Israel to be saved. The Holy Spirit was with him, ²⁶and he had been assured by the Holy Spirit that he would not die before he had seen the Lord's promised Messiah. ²⁷Led by the Spirit, Simeon went into the Temple. When the parents brought the child Jesus into the Temple to do for him what the Law required, ²⁸Simeon took the child in his arms, and gave thanks to God:

> ²⁹"Now, Lord, you have kept your promise,
> And you may let your servant go in peace.
> ³⁰For with my own eyes I have seen your salvation,
> ³¹Which you have made ready in the presence of all peoples:
> ³²A light to reveal your way to the Gentiles,
> And to give glory to your people Israel."

³³The child's father and mother were amazed at the things Simeon said about him. ³⁴Simeon blessed them and said to Mary, his mother: "This child is chosen by God for the destruction and the salvation of many in Israel; he will be a sign from God which many people will speak against, ³⁵and so reveal their secret thoughts. And sorrow, like a sharp sword, will break your own heart."

³⁶There was a prophetess named Anna, daughter of Phanuel, of the tribe of Asher. She was an old woman who had been married for seven years, ³⁷and then had been a widow for

eighty-four years. She never left the Temple; day and night she worshiped God, fasting and praying. ³⁸That very same hour she arrived and gave thanks to God, and spoke about the child to all who were waiting for God to redeem Jerusalem.

In the final episode of the infancy narrative (2:41–52), Jesus and his parents go to Jerusalem on the Passover pilgrimage. There the twelve-year-old Jesus discusses points of Old Testament interpretation with the Jewish scholars and wins their admiration.

This section of Luke's Gospel ends as it began in the Temple at Jerusalem. Each event in the Temple significantly advances the story of salvation. Mary is again portrayed as the faithful and reflective disciple of her own son, the model of the true believer.

■ *Reflection*

How is the news of Jesus' presence in the world greeted by contemporary society?

The Return to Nazareth

³⁹When they finished doing all that was required by the law of the Lord, they returned to Galilee, to their home town of Nazareth. ⁴⁰And the child grew and became strong; he was full of wisdom, and God's blessings were with him.

⁴¹Every year Jesus' parents went to Jerusalem for the Feast of Passover. ⁴²When Jesus was twelve years old, they went to the feast as usual. ⁴³When the days of the feast were over, they started back home, but the boy Jesus stayed in Jerusalem. His parents did not know this; ⁴⁴they thought that he was with the group, so they traveled a whole day, and then started

looking for him among their relatives and friends. ⁴⁵They did not find him, so they went back to Jerusalem looking for him. ⁴⁶On the third day they found him in the Temple, sitting with the Jewish teachers, listening to them and asking questions. ⁴⁷All who heard him were amazed at his intelligent answers. ⁴⁸His parents were amazed when they saw him, and his mother said to him, "Son, why did you do this to us? Your father and I have been terribly worried trying to find you." ⁴⁹He answered them, "Why did you have to look for me? Didn't you know that I had to be in my Father's house?" ⁵⁰But they did not understand what he said to them.

⁵¹So Jesus went back with them to Nazareth, where he was obedient to them. His mother treasured all these things in her heart. ⁵²And Jesus grew up, both in body and in wisdom, gaining favor with God and men.

■ Discussion

1. What similarities and differences are there in the announcements of John's and Jesus' births?
2. How do the hymns in 1:47–55 and 1:68–79 describe God in relation to his people?
3. What picture of Mary emerges in chapters 1 and 2?
4. How does the infancy narrative prepare us for the story of Jesus as an adult?
5. What sources does Luke use to establish the identity of Jesus? Is there more than one way to describe Jesus' identity?

■ Prayer and Meditation

"Those who guard the city are shouting,
  shouting together for joy.
They can see with their own eyes
  the return of the LORD to Zion.
Break into shouts of joy,
  you ruins of Jerusalem!
The LORD will rescue his city
  and comfort his people.
The LORD will use his holy power;
  he will save his people,
  and all the world will see it."

Isaiah 52:8–10

Son of God and Prophet/ Powerful in Word and Deed ——————— Luke 3:1—6:19

Luke's presentation of John the Baptist's preaching in 3:1—6 emphasizes John's subordination to Jesus and his task of preparing the way for Jesus. The fifteenth year of the emperor Tiberius was A.D. 28—29. By mentioning the various rulers and officials, Luke places the lives of John and Jesus in the framework of world history. Furthermore, all these characters except Lysanias are mentioned later in the Gospel, and so they will need no introduction them.

Luke 3:4—6, contains a quotation from Isaiah 40:3—5. The Old Testament passage is taken from that part of the book of Isaiah that looks forward to Isarel's return from exile in Babylon in 537 B.C. In the setting of the long journey back from Babylon to Jerusalem, the idea is that God will make the way smooth and all people will see his saving power. In the New Testament John is the voice and Jesus is the saving power of God.

Luke 3:7—9 is the first sample of John's preaching. The audience is the crowd that came out to the wilderness. The "wrath to come" refers to God's intervention in world history and the establishment of his kingship over all creation. This will be preceded by a period of intense testing and suffering.

John gives the crowd three warnings. Merely listening to John's preaching (3:7b–8a) cannot save them, nor can physical membership alone in the people descended from Abraham (3:8b). They cannot afford to waste time and put off their repentance (3:9).

Besides the warnings, John provided some positive advice to various groups: the crowds (3:10–11), the tax collectors (3:12–13), and the soldiers (3:14). The crowds are urged to be unselfish and to share with others, while the tax collectors and soldiers are told to be honest and not to use their position to gain personal advantage.

The third sample of John's preaching in 3:15–18 contrasts his baptism and the new baptism brought by Jesus. This contrast is one of the means Luke used to describe the relation between John and Jesus. John places himself in a position of servitude to the one who is to come after. As he was aware that some believed him to be the Messiah, this passage attributes to John great humility.

The section on John the Baptist ends with a brief report about his imprisonment in 3:19–20. The Herod mentioned in 3:19 is Herod Antipas, the ruler of Galilee from 4 B.C. to A.D. 39 and the son of Herod the Great. Herodias had been married to Herod Antipas' half brother named Herod also.

Before telling us about Jesus' public activity, Luke identifies Jesus as the Son of God in three different passages: the baptism (3:21–22), the genealogy (3:23–38), and the testing or temptation (4:1–13). That Jesus was baptized by John is undoubtedly a historical fact. To appreciate Luke's understanding of that event, it is important to pay attention to the details in 3:21–22 in comparison with Matthew 3:13–17 and Mark 1:9–11.

Here is a key event during which we see two elements recurring: Jesus prays following his baptism, and the Holy Spirit is present, this time in a "bodily form."

The Preaching of John the Baptist
(Also Matt. 3.1–12; Mark 1.1–8; John 1.19–28)

3 It was the fifteenth year of the rule of Emperor Tiberius; Pontius Pilate was governor of Judea, Herod was ruler of Galilee, and his brother Philip ruler of the territory of Iturea and Trachonitis; Lysanias was ruler of Abilene, ²and Annas and Caiaphas were high priests. It was at this time that the word of God came to John, the son of Zechariah, in the desert. ³So John went throughout the whole territory of the Jordan river. "Turn away from your sins and be baptized," he preached, "and God will forgive your sins." ⁴As the prophet Isaiah had written in his book:

> "Someone is shouting in the desert:
> 'Get the Lord's road ready for him,
> Make a straight path for him to travel!
> ⁵All low places must be filled up,
> All hills and mountains leveled off;
> The winding roads must be made straight,
> The rough paths made smooth;
> ⁶And all mankind will see God's salvation!' "

⁷Crowds of people came out to John to be baptized by him. "You snakes!" he said to them. "Who told you that you could escape from God's wrath that is about to come? ⁸Do the things that will show that you have turned from your sins. And don't start saying among yourselves, 'Abraham is our ancestor.' I tell you that God can take these rocks and make descendants for Abraham! ⁹The ax is ready to

cut the trees down at the roots; every tree that does not bear good fruit will be cut down and thrown in the fire." ¹⁰The people asked him, "What are we to do, then?" ¹¹He answered, "Whoever has two shirts must give one to the man who has none, and whoever has food must share it." ¹²Some tax collectors came to be baptized, and they asked him, "Teacher, what are we to do?" ¹³"Don't collect more than is legal," he told them. ¹⁴Some soldiers also asked him, "What about us? What are we to do?" He said to them, "Don't take money from anyone by force or by false charges; be content with your pay."

¹⁵People's hopes began to rise and they began to wonder about John, thinking that perhaps he might be the Messiah. ¹⁶So John said to all of them: "I baptize you with water, but one who is much greater than I is coming. I am not good enough even to untie his sandals. He will baptize you with the Holy Spirit and fire. ¹⁷He has his winnowing-shovel with him, to thresh out all the grain and gather the wheat into his barn; but he will burn the chaff in a fire that never goes out!"

¹⁸In many different ways John urged the people as he preached the Good News to them. ¹⁹But John spoke against Governor Herod, because he had married Herodias, his brother's wife, and had done many other evil things. ²⁰Then Herod did an even worse thing by putting John in prison.

²¹After all the people had been baptized, Jesus also was baptized. While he was praying, heaven was opened, ²²and the Holy Spirit came down upon him in bodily form, like a dove. And a voice came from heaven: "You are my own dear Son. I am well pleased with you."

The second passage identifying Jesus as the Son of God is the list of Jesus' ancestors in 3:23–38. It traces Jesus' genealogy back to Adam and ultimately to God. Matthew's genealogy traces Jesus' ancestry back to Abraham, the father of the Hebrew nation. Luke continues the lineage back to Adam, the father of all humankind and to God the creator. The implication to be drawn is that all people are God's children, and that Jesus is not only a Jew come to save the Jews.

The old suggestion that Luke gives Jesus' descent through Mary and Matthew gives it through Joseph, is based on very slender evidence. But it does call attention to an important difference between Matthew 1—2 and Luke 1—2. The focus of attention in Matthew is clearly Joseph, whereas Luke centers on the activities and thoughts of Mary.

The Ancestors of Jesus
(Also Matt. 1.1–17)

[23]When Jesus began his work he was about thirty years old; he was the son, so people thought, of Joseph, who was the son of Heli, [24]the son of Matthat, the son of Levi, the son of Melchi, the son of Jannai, the son of Joseph, [25]the son of Mattathias, the son of Amos, the son of Nahum, the son of Esli, the son of Naggai, [26]the son of Maath, the son of Mattathias, the son of Semein, the son of Josech, the son of Joda, [27]the son of Joanan, the son of Rhesa, the son of Zerubbabel, the son of Shealtiel, the son of Neri, [28]the son of Melchi, the son of Addi, the son of Cosam, the son of Elmadam, the son of Er, [29]the son of Joshua, the son of Eliezer, the son of Jorim, the son of Matthat, the son of Levi, [30]the son of Simeon, the son of Judah, the son of Joseph, the son of Jonam, the son of

Eliakim, ³¹the son of Melea, the son of Menna, the son of Mattatha, the son of Nathan, the son of David, ³²the son of Jesse, the son of Obed, the son of Boaz, the son of Salmon, the son of Nahshon, ³³the son of Amminadab, the son of Admin, the son of Arni, the son of Hezron, the son of Perez, the son of Judah, ³⁴the son of Jacob, the son of Isaac, the son of Abraham, the son of Terah, the son of Nahor, ³⁵the son of Serug, the son of Reu, the son of Peleg, the son of Eber, the son of Shelah, ³⁶the son of Cainan, the son of Arphaxad, the son of Shem, the son of Noah, the son of Lamech, ³⁷the son of Methuselah, the son of Enoch, the son of Jared, the son of Mahalaleel, the son of Cainan, ³⁸the son of Enos, the son of Seth, the son of Adam, the son of God.

The Son Is Tested

The so-called temptation of Jesus is better described as the testing of God's Son prior to his public ministry. The Spirit is present here again at an important part of Jesus' life. The fact that all of Jesus' responses are taken from the Old Testament book of Deuteronomy implies that Jesus is repeating the testing of Israel in the wilderness after the escape from Egypt. But whereas Israel of old failed the test, Jesus as God's Son succeeds.

The actual testing takes the form of a debate between the devil and Jesus. Three times Jesus is urged to prove his divine sonship ("If you are God's Son . . ."), and three times he refuses to do so. Having been defeated in debate with Jesus, the devil leaves the scene until the opportune time at the very beginning of the passion story in Luke 22:3.

The Temptation of Jesus
(Also Matt. 4.1−11; Mark 1.12−13)

4 Jesus returned from the Jordan full of the Holy Spirit, and was led by the Spirit into the desert, ²where he was tempted by the Devil for forty days. He ate nothing all that time, so that he was hungry when it was over.

³The Devil said to him, "If you are God's Son, order this stone to turn into bread." ⁴Jesus answered, "The scripture says, 'Man cannot live on bread alone.' "

⁵Then the Devil took him up and showed him in a second all the kingdoms of the world. ⁶"I will give you all this power, and all this wealth," the Devil told him. "It was all handed over to me and I can give it to anyone I choose. ⁷All this will be yours, then, if you kneel down before me." ⁸Jesus answered, "The scripture says, "Worship the Lord your God and serve only him!' "

⁹Then the Devil took him to Jerusalem and set him on the highest point of the Temple, and said to him, "If you are God's Son, throw yourself down from here. ¹⁰For the scripture says, 'God will order his angels to take good care of you.' ¹¹It also says, 'They will hold you up with their hands so that you will not even hurt your feet on the stones.' " ¹²Jesus answered him, "The scripture says, 'You must not put the Lord your God to the test,' " ¹³When the Devil finished tempting Jesus in every way, he left him for a while.

Ministry in Galilee

The summary of Jesus' movements in 4:14–15 explains how he returned from the wilderness to his home area in Galilee. The story of Jesus' rejection at Nazareth in 4:16–30 introduces the recurring theme in Luke's Gospel: the rejection of Jesus by his contemporaries and their ultimate aim, his death. It is quite likely on historical grounds that Jesus preached in the synagogue at Nazareth and that he experienced rejection and hostility from his fellow townspeople. But the account of this event seems to have been shaped rather extensively by Luke himself in order to better illustrate its true significance.

The passage contains an introduction in 4:16a and a conclusion in 4:30. The body of the account consists of two incidents, each narrating an action by Jesus and the people's reaction to it. Jesus' first action (4:16b–21) involves reading an Old Testament passage and commenting on it. Anyone of sufficient learning could be invited to read a Scripture passage and explain it, and so Jesus' action is not at all extraordinary. The Old Testament quotation joins Isaiah 61:1–2 and 58:6. Jesus proclaims that the Scripture passage was fulfilled that day. The crowd's first reaction (4:22) is a mixture of amazement and puzzlement.

Jesus' second action (4:23–27) is an explanation of why he refuses to perform the miracles in Nazareth that he did in Capernaum. But we really have not been told anything about Jesus' miracles in Capernaum.

The proverb about prophets not being accepted in their own country leads Jesus to cite the example of two Old Testament prophets who ministered to non-Jews. Luke continues to suggest the theme that Jesus is sent to save all nations. The presence of this theme reflects the controversies between Jewish and gentile Christians in the apostolic Church. Luke is here not attempting to convert those of Jewish ancestry so much as to offer consolation to the non-Jews in the Church. The crowd's very hostile reaction (4:28–29) is the first in a whole series of negative responses to Jesus in the Gospel.

■ *Reflection*

Is each follower of Christ called to be a prophet? How would a contemporary prophet react in today's Church?

Jesus Begins His Work in Galilee
(Also Matt. 4.12–17; Mark 1.14–15)

¹⁴Then Jesus returned to Galilee, and the power of the Holy Spirit was with him. The news about him spread throughout all that territory. ¹⁵He taught in their synagogues and was praised by all.

¹⁶Then Jesus went to Nazareth, where he had been brought up, and on the Sabbath day he went as usual to the synagogue. He stood up to read the Scriptures, ¹⁷and was handed the book of the prophet Isaiah. He unrolled the scroll and found the place where it is written:
¹⁸"The Spirit of the Lord is upon me.
He has anointed me to preach the Good News to the poor,
He has sent me to proclaim liberty to the captives,
And recovery of sight to the blind,
To set free the oppressed,
¹⁹To announce the year when the Lord will save his people!"
²⁰Jesus rolled up the scroll, gave it back to the attendant, and sat down. All the people in

the synagogue had their eyes fixed on him. [21]He began speaking to them: "This passage of scripture has come true today, as you heard it being read." [22]They were all well impressed with him, and marveled at the beautiful words that he spoke. They said, "Isn't he the son of Joseph?" [23]He said to them: "I am sure that you will quote the proverb to me, 'Doctor, heal yourself.' You will also say to me, 'Do here in your own home town the same things we were told happened in Capernaum,' [24]I tell you this," Jesus added: "A prophet is never welcomed in his own home town. [25]Listen to me: it is true that there were many widows in Israel during the time of Elijah, when there was no rain for three and a half years and there was a great famine throughout the whole land. [26]Yet Elijah was not sent to a single one of them, but only to a widow of Zarephath, in the territory of Sidon. [27]And there were many lepers in Israel during the time of the prophet Elisha; yet not one of them was made clean, but only Naaman the Syrian." [28]All the people in the synagogue were filled with anger when they heard this. [29]They rose up, dragged Jesus out of town, and took him to the top of the hill on which their town was built, to throw him over the cliff. [30]But he walked through the middle of the crowd and went his way.

Powerful in Word and Deed

After making clear Jesus' identity as the Son of God and prophet, Luke describes Jesus' activities as teacher and healer in 4:31—6:19. In this section he follows Mark 1:21—3:19 very closely. In 4:31—37 the public astonishment at Jesus' teaching at the synagogue at Capernaum on the Sabbath is interrupted by his exorcism of a demon, which in turn confirms the power of his teaching. Jesus is powerful not only in word but in deed. The healing of Simon Peter's mother-in-law underscores the extraordinary power of Jesus. The cure was so total and so quick that the woman could get up and serve dinner. The summary in 4:40–41 indicates that Jesus performed more miracles than are described in the Gospel. The fact that the demons recognized Jesus as the Son of God and Messiah shows that the healings are part of the larger struggle between the forces of Satan and Jesus.

³¹Then Jesus went to Capernaum, a town in Galilee, where he taught the people on the Sabbath. ³²They were all amazed at the way he taught, for his words had authority. ³³There was a man in the synagogue who had the spirit of an evil demon in him; he screamed out in a loud voice: ³⁴"Ah! What do you want with us, Jesus of Nazareth? Are you here to destroy us? I know who you are: you are God's holy messenger!" ³⁵Jesus commanded the spirit: "Be quiet, and come out of the man!" The demon threw the man down in front of them all, and went out of him without doing him any harm. ³⁶Everyone was amazed, and they said to one another: "What kind of word is this? With authority and power this man gives orders to the evil spirits, and they come out!" ³⁷And the report about Jesus spread everywhere in that region.

³⁸Jesus left the synagogue and went to Simon's home. Simon's mother-in-law was sick with a high fever, and they spoke to Jesus about her. ³⁹He went and stood at her bedside, and gave a command to the fever. The fever left her and she got up at once and began to wait on them.

⁴⁰After sunset, all who had friends who were sick with various diseases brought them to Jesus; he placed his hands on every one of them and healed them all. ⁴¹Demons, also, went out from many people screaming, "You are the Son of God!" Jesus commanded them and would not let them speak, because they knew that he was the Messiah.

The Call

The power of Jesus in word and deed is illustrated very dramatically in the call of the disciples. His proclamation of the kingdom of God (4:42–44) is described as the "word of God" in 5:1, and the power of that word is demonstrated by the miraculous catch of fish that results from the disciples' obeying that word. From the very beginning of their time with Jesus, Simon and the others witness the power of Jesus expressed in both word and deed. They are invited to share in Jesus' life-giving ministry (5:10). The sacrifice made by the disciples in leaving everything to follow Jesus should not be passed over lightly. Fishing was a major industry in Galilee, and these first disciples had their own boats and nets. The attraction of Jesus must have been very powerful to have led them to leave their stable and profitable business and their families.

A leper healed by Jesus' touch and word in 5:12–16 suffered from a skin disease, not necessarily what today is called Hansen's disease. In order to be restored to full participation in the life of the Jewish commmunity, the healed man was instructed to comply with the rules laid down in Leviticus 14. The story of his healing increased public enthusiasm for Jesus. At this decisive moment in his public ministry, Jesus withdrew to the wilderness for prayer.

⁴²At daybreak Jesus left the town and went off to a lonely place. The people started looking for him, and when they found him they tried to keep him from leaving. ⁴³But he said to them, "I must preach the Good News of the Kingdom of God in other towns also, for that is what God sent me to do." ⁴⁴So he preached in the synagogues of Judea.

Jesus Calls the First Disciples
(Also Matt. 4.18–22; Mark 1.16–20)

5 One time Jesus was standing on the shore of Lake Gennesaret while the people pushed their way up to him to listen to the word of God. ²He saw two boats pulled up on the beach; the fishermen had left them and gone off to wash the nets. ³Jesus got into one of the boats—it belonged to Simon—and asked him to push off a little from the shore. Jesus sat in the boat and taught the crowd.

⁴When he finished speaking, he said to Simon, "Push the boat out further to the deep water, and you and your partners let your nets down for a catch." ⁵"Master," Simon answered, "we worked hard all night long and caught nothing. But if you say so, I will let down the nets." ⁶They let the nets down and caught such a large number of fish that the nets were about to break. ⁷So they motioned to their partners in the other boat to come and help them. They came and filled both boats so full of fish that they were about to sink. ⁸When Simon Peter saw what had happened, he fell on his knees before Jesus and said, "Go away from me, Lord, for I am a sinful man!" ⁹He and all the others with him were amazed at the large number of fish they had caught. ¹⁰The

same was true of Simon's partners, James and John, the sons of Zebedee. Jesus said to Simon, "Don't be afraid; from now on you will be catching men." ¹¹They pulled the boats on the beach, left everything, and followed Jesus.

Jesus Heals a Man
(Also Matt. 8.1–4; Mark 1.40–45

¹²Once Jesus was in a certain town where there was a man who was covered with leprosy. When he saw Jesus, he fell on his face before him and begged, "Sir, if you want to, you can make me clean!" ¹³Jesus reached out and touched him. "I do want to," he said. "Be clean!" At once the leprosy left the man. ¹⁴Jesus ordered him, "Don't tell this to anyone, but go straight to the priest and let him examine you; then offer the sacrifice, as Moses ordered, to prove to everyone that you are now clean." ¹⁵But the news about Jesus spread all the more widely, and crowds of people came to hear him and be healed from their diseases. ¹⁶But he would go away to lonely places, where he prayed.

Conflicts

The theme of Jesus' power in word and deed is continued in the five conflict stories or controversies in 5:17–6:11. The controversy over Jesus' power to forgive sins consists of a healing story (5:18–19, 24b–26) and a debate (5:20–24a). The power of Jesus' word is confirmed by his ability to heal a paralyzed man.

The controversy in 5:27–32 involves the kinds of people with whom Jesus associated. Tax collectors like Levi were suspected of dishonesty and collaboration with the Romans, and "sinners" had bad reputations and paid no attention to the observance of the Old Testament law. To such people Jesus had been sent to preach the good news of God's kingdom.

The failure of Jesus' disciples to observe fasts (5:33–39) is the occasion for calling attention to the special character of the time of Jesus. It is the time of the bridegroom, the time in which a patchwork of old and new will not suffice, a time of joy and newness. The disciples' action in plucking grain on the Sabbath (6:1–5) is defended by appeal to the example of David in 1 Samuel 21:1–6 and to the authority of the Son of Man as Lord of the Sabbath. The fifth and last controversy (6:6–11) also concerns work on the Sabbath. In this case Jesus defends his action in healing the man with the withered hand on the ground that it is acceptable to do good and to save life on the Sabbath.

The five controversies all introduce the opponents of Jesus and show how he outwitted them in debate. They also provide precedents or examples from the life of Jesus on such controversial matters as the forgiveness of sins, associating with outsiders, fasting, and observing the Sabbath rest. Finally, they make some startling claims about Jesus: he can forgive sins; he was sent to sinners; he is the bridegroom; he is the Lord of the Sabbath; he is the authoritative interpreter of the Old Testament.

Jesus Heals a Paralyzed Man
(Also Matt. 9.1–8; Mark 2.1–12)

¹⁷One day when Jesus was teaching some Pharisees and teachers of the Law were sitting there who had come from every town in Galilee and Judea, and from Jerusalem. The power of the Lord was present for Jesus to heal the sick. ¹⁸Some men came carrying a paralyzed man on

a bed, and they tried to take him into the house and lay him before Jesus. [19]Because of the crowd, however, they could find no way to take him in. So they carried him up on the roof, made an opening in the tiles, and let him down on his bed into the middle of the group in front of Jesus. [20]When Jesus saw how much faith they had, he said to the man, "Your sins are forgiven you, my friend." [21]The teachers of the Law and the Pharisees began to say to themselves: "Who is this man who speaks against God in this way? No man can forgive sins; God alone can!" [22]Jesus knew their thoughts and said to them: "Why do you think such things? [23]Is it easier to say, 'Your sins are forgiven you,' or to say, 'Get up and walk'? [24]I will prove to you, then, that the Son of Man has authority on earth to forgive sins." So he said to the paralyzed man, "I tell you, get up, pick up your bed, and go home!" [25]At once the man got up before them all, took the bed he had been lying on, and went home, praising God. [26]They were all completely amazed! Full of fear, they praised God, saying, "What marvelous things we have seen today!"

Jesus Calls Levi

[27]After this, Jesus went out and saw a tax collector named Levi, sitting in his office. Jesus said to him, "Follow me." [28]Levi got up, left everything, and followed him.

[29]Then Levi had a big feast in his house for Jesus, and there was a large number of tax collectors and other people sitting with them. [30]Some Pharisees and teachers of the Law who belonged to their group complained to Jesus' disciples. "Why do you eat and drink with tax

collectors and outcasts?'' they asked. [31]Jesus answered them: ''People who are well do not need a doctor, but only those who are sick. [32]I have not come to call the respectable people to repent, but the outcasts.''

The Question About Fasting
(Also Matt. 9.14—17; Mark 2.18—22)

[33]Some people said to Jesus, ''The disciples of John fast frequently and offer up prayers, and the disciples of the Pharisees do the same; but your disciples eat and drink.'' [34]Jesus answered: ''Do you think you can make the guests at a wedding party go without food as long as the bridegroom is with them? Of course not! [35]But the time will come when the bridegroom will be taken away from them, and they will go without food in those days.''

[36]Jesus told them this parable also: ''No one tears a piece off a new coat to patch up an old coat. If he does, he will have torn the new coat, and the piece of new cloth will not match the old. [37]Nor does anyone pour new wine into used wineskins. If he does, the new wine will burst the skins, the wine will pour out, and the skins will be ruined. [38]No! New wine should be poured into fresh skins! [39]And no one wants new wine after drinking old wine. 'The old is better,' he says.''

The Question About the Sabbath
(Also Matt. 12.1—8; Mark 2.23—28)

6 Jesus was walking through some wheat fields on a Sabbath day. His disciples began to pick the heads of wheat, rub them in their hands, and eat the grain. [2]Some

Pharisees said, "Why are you doing what our Law says you cannot do on the Sabbath?" ³Jesus answered them: "Haven't you read what David did when he and his men were hungry? ⁴He went into the house of God, took the bread offered to God, ate it, and gave it also to his men. Yet it is against our Law for anyone to eat it except the priests." ⁵And Jesus added, "The Son of Man is Lord of the Sabbath."

The Man with a Paralyzed Hand
(Also Matt. 12.9—14; Mark 3.1—6)

⁶On another Sabbath Jesus went into a synagogue and taught. A man was there whose right hand was crippled. ⁷Some teachers of the Law and Pharisees wanted some reason to accuse Jesus of doing wrong; so they watched him very closely to see if he would cure anyone on the Sabbath. ⁸But Jesus knew their thoughts and said to the man with the crippled hand, "Stand up and come here to the front." The man got up and stood there. ⁹Then Jesus said to them: "I ask you: What does our Law allow us to do on the Sabbath? To help or to harm? To save a man's life or destroy it?" ¹⁰He looked around at them all, then said to the man, "Stretch out your hand." He did so, and his hand became well again. ¹¹But they were filled with rage and began to discuss among themselves what they could do to Jesus.

The Choice of the Twelve

The momentous character of the choice of the twelve apostles (6:12—16) is underlined by the statement that it was preceded by a night of prayer. For Luke the choice of the twelve apostles was especially important, since the apostles as witnesses of Jesus' words and deeds were the principles of continuity between Jesus and the Church.

In 6:17–19 the scene for the first major sample of Jesus' teaching is set. It is a level place or plain, and great crowds have gathered to experience the healing power of Jesus. The Sermon on the Plain in 6:20–49 will manifest the power of his word.

■ *Reflection*

How does the Church today bear witness to Jesus' words and deeds?

How is the action of the Holy Spirit evident in the Church today? in my life?

Jesus Chooses the Twelve Apostles
(Also Matt. 10.1–4; Mark 3.13–19)

¹²At that time Jesus went up a hill to pray, and spent the whole night there praying to God. ¹³When day came he called his disciples to him and chose twelve of them, whom he named apostles: ¹⁴Simon (whom he also named Peter) and his brother Andrew, James and John, Philip and Bartholomew, ¹⁵Matthew and Thomas, James the son of Alphaeus and Simon (who was called the patriot), ¹⁶Judas the son of James and Judas Iscariot, who became the traitor.

Jesus Teaches and Heals
(Also Matt. 4.23–25)

¹⁷Coming down from the hill with them, Jesus stood on a level place with a large number of his disciples. A great crowd of people was there from all over Judea, and from Jerusalem, and from the coast cities of Tyre and Sidon; ¹⁸they came to hear him and to be

healed of their diseases. Those who were troubled by evil spirits also came and were healed. ¹⁹All the people tried to touch him, for power was going out from him and healing them all.

■ Discussion

1. Reread the three Son-of-God passages: the baptism (3:21–22); the genealogy (3:23–38); and the testing (4:1–13). How is Jesus' divine sonship brought out in each passage?
2. What is the role of the Holy Spirit in these three passages?
3. How is the significance of Jesus for all humanity (not simply for Israel) made clear in these three passages?
4. Is it correct to call Jesus a prophet?
5. Based on the events in Luke's Gospel to this point, can you see any reason to predict Jesus' rejection and execution in Jerusalem?

■ Prayer and Meditation

"A voice cries out,
'Prepare in the wilderness a road for the LORD!
    Clear the way in the desert for our God!
Fill every valley;
    level every mountain.
The hills will become a plain,
    and the rough country will be made smooth.
Then the glory of the LORD will be revealed,
    and all mankind will see it.
The LORD himself has promised this.' "

Isaiah 40:3–5

Teacher and Healer/ Revelation and Misunderstanding

_____ Luke 6:20—9:50

The Sermon on the Plain is Luke's equivalent to Matthew's Sermon on the Mount. In Luke the plain, or level place, is where Jesus meets the people. The Sermon on the Plain consists of blessings and woes (6:20–26), positive teachings on love (6:27–38), and warnings against false teachers (6:39–49).

The four blessings in 6:20–23 declare certain groups of people to be privileged recipients of God's special gifts. God is on their side, not against them. When the coming of God's kingdom brings about a dramatic reversal of status, these people will be exalted.

The four woes in 6:24–26 obviously parallel the blessings in form and content. Luke has already identified Jesus as the Messiah who has come to save the poor and lowly. The contrast between human justice and God's justice, brought out before in references to the Old Testament, is here emphasized in Jesus' new teachings.

The positive teachings on love (6:27–38) include the basic principle (6:27–28), four extreme examples (6:29–30), and three motives (6:31–38). The basic principle of loving one's enemies goes beyond the Old Testament's teaching about loving one's neighbor.

The four cases in 6:29–30 give extreme examples of how the principle of loving one's enemies can shape our lives and change our behavior patterns. In each instance our instinctive behavior is challenged. The three motives in 6:31–38 are acting toward other people in a way that we wish they would act toward us (6:31), imitating the example of God (6:32–36), and treating others in a way we hope to be treated (6:37–38).

The first major sample of Jesus' teaching concludes with warnings against false teachers (6:39–49). Many of these sayings probably had their original setting in Jesus' controversies with the Pharisees and scribes, but in their Lukan context they may refer to false teachers within the Christian community who depart from Jesus the teacher (6:40).

The saying about the fruit tree in 6:43–44 is a comment on the relation between actions and internal disposition. Like the other sayings in this sequence, it illustrates the contrast between those who are genuine religious leaders or teachers, and those who do not understand the message of Jesus.

■ *Reflection*

How can the Beatitudes be rephrased to be more applicable to today's society?

Happiness and Sorrow
(Also Matt. 5.1–12)

[20]Jesus looked at his disciples and said:
    "Happy are you poor:
        the Kingdom of God is yours!
    [21]"Happy are you who are hungry now:
        you will be filled!
    "Happy are you who weep now:
        you will laugh!

²²"Happy are you when men hate you, and reject you, and insult you, and say that you are evil, because of the Son of Man! ²³Be happy when that happens, and dance for joy, for a great reward is kept for you in heaven. For their ancestors did the very same things to the prophets.

²⁴"But how terrible for you who are rich
now:
you have had your easy life!
²⁵"How terrible for you who are full
now:
you will go hungry!
"How terrible for you who laugh now:
you will mourn and weep!

²⁶"How terrible when all men speak well of you; for their ancestors said the very same things to the false prophets."

Love for Enemies
(Also Matt. 5.38–48; 7.12a)

²⁷"But I tell you who hear me: Love your enemies, do good to those who hate you, ²⁸bless those who curse you, and pray for those who mistreat you. ²⁹If anyone hits you on the cheek, let him hit the other one too; if someone takes your coat, let him have your shirt as well. ³⁰Give to everyone who asks you for something, and when someone takes what is yours, do not ask for it back. ³¹Do for others just what you want them to do for you.

³²"If you love only the people who love you, why should you expect a blessing? Even sinners love those who love them! ³³And if you do good only to those who do good to you, why should you expect a blessing? Even sinners do that! ³⁴And if you lend only to those from whom

you hope to get it back, why should you expect a blessing? Even sinners lend to sinners, to get back the same amount! [35]No! Love your enemies and do good to them; lend and expect nothing back. You will have a great reward, and you will be sons of the Most High God. For he is good to the ungrateful and the wicked. [36]Be merciful, just as your Father is merciful.''

Judging Others
(Also Matt. 7.1–5)

[37]''Do not judge others, and God will not judge you; do not condemn others, and God will not condemn you; forgive others, and God will forgive you. [38]Give to others, and God will give to you: you will receive a full measure, a generous helping, poured into your hands—all that you can hold. The measure you use for others is the one God will use for you.''

[39]And Jesus told them this parable: ''One blind man cannot lead another one; if he does, both will fall into a ditch. [40]No pupil is greater than his teacher; but every pupil, when he has completed his training, will be like his teacher.

[41]''Why do you look at the speck in your brother's eye, but pay no attention to the log in your own eye? [42]How can you say to your brother, 'Please, brother, let me take that speck out of your eye,' yet not even see the log in your own eye? You impostor! Take the log out of your own eye first, and then you will be able to see and take the speck out of your brother's eye.''

A Tree and Its Fruit
(Also Matt. 7.16–20; 12.33–35)

[43]"A healthy tree does not bear bad fruit, nor does a poor tree bear good fruit. [44]Every tree is known by the fruit it bears; you do not pick figs from thorn bushes, or gather grapes from bramble bushes. [45]A good man brings good out of the treasure of good things in his heart; a bad man brings bad out of his treasure of bad things. For a man's mouth speaks what his heart is full of."

The Two House Builders
(Also Matt. 7.24–27)

[46]"Why do you call me, 'Lord, Lord,' and don't do what I tell you? [47]Everyone who comes to me, and listens to my words, and obeys them—I will show you what he is like. [48]He is like a man who built a house: he dug deep and laid the foundation on the rock. The river flooded over and hit that house but it could not shake it, because the house had been well built. [49]But the one who hears my words and does not obey them is like a man who built a house on the ground without laying a foundation; when the flood hit that house it fell at once—what a terrible crash that was!"

The Centurion's Servant

Having illustrated Jesus' power as a teacher in the Sermon on the Plain, Luke now shows Jesus' power as a healer in the healing of the centurion's servant in 7:1–10. Similar stories appear in Matthew 8 and John 4. The characteristic feature of Luke's account is its emphasis on the centurion's attitude toward Jesus. The centurion was a non-Jew and apparently the commander of the Roman military force stationed in Capernaum. He was very friendly to the Jews and compassionate toward his sick servant.

The centurion communicated with Jesus through the Jewish elders as a sign of respect for protocol in dealing with the religious officials in the district. He also communicated a sense of unworthiness in the presence of one who had a reputation as a great teacher and healer. Besides his sense of unworthiness, the centurion also probably wanted to avoid putting Jesus in bad standing with the Pharisees, who might object to his associating with non-Jews. The centurion provides a model for all non-Jews who come to believe in the power of Jesus. His faith is not supported by national tradition, yet it is a strong faith based on the witness of Jesus' miraculous deeds and preaching.

Jesus Heals a Roman Officer's Servant
(Also Matt. 8.5–13)

7 When Jesus had finished saying all these things to the people, he went to Capernaum. ²A Roman officer there had a servant who was very dear to him; the man was sick and about to die. ³When the officer heard about Jesus, he sent to him some Jewish elders to ask him to come and heal his servant. ⁴They came to Jesus and begged him earnestly: "This man really deserves your help. ⁵He loves our people and he himself built a synagogue for us." ⁶So Jesus went with them. He was not far from the house when the officer sent friends to tell him: "Sir, don't trouble yourself. I do not deserve to have you come into my house, ⁷neither do I consider myself worthy to come to you in person. Just give the order and my servant will get well. ⁸I, too, am a man placed under the authority of superior officers, and I have soldiers under me. I order this one, 'Go!' and he goes; I order that one, 'Come!' and he comes; and I order my slave, 'Do this!' and he does it." ⁹Jesus was surprised when he heard this; he turned around and said to the crowd following him, "I have never found such faith as this, I tell you, not even in Israel!" ¹⁰The messengers went back to the officer's house and found his servant well.

The Widow's Son

In the story of the widow's son at Nain (7:11–17), an even greater act of power confirms the power of Jesus' teaching and points toward the resurrection of Jesus as the ground for all hope for resurrected life.

In the time of Jesus, families existed only if there was a man to be the head of the household. The widow, without her only son, would be without a family. No one would provide for and protect her and her daughters, unless she had relatives to take her in. Jesus' decision to intervene is an example both of his compassion and of his fulfilling the mission to bring good news to the poor and the lowly.

The widow's son is raised to life by the power of Jesus' word. The same language is used later on to describe Jesus' own resurrection. The relation between the two events becomes more apparent in the description of the reaction of the crowd.

Jesus Raises a Widow's Son

¹¹Soon afterward Jesus went to a town named Nain; his disciples and a large crowd went with him. ¹²Just as he arrived at the gate of the town, a funeral procession was coming

out. The dead man was the only son of a woman who was a widow, and a large crowd from the city was with her. ¹³When the Lord saw her his heart was filled with pity for her and he said to her, "Don't cry." ¹⁴Then he walked over and touched the coffin, and the men carrying it stopped. Jesus said, "Young man! Get up, I tell you!" ¹⁵The dead man sat up and began to talk, and Jesus gave him back to his mother. ¹⁶Everyone was filled with fear, and they praised God: "A great prophet has appeared among us!" and, "God has come to save his people!" ¹⁷This news about Jesus went out through all of Judea and the surrounding territory.

Jesus and John

The relationship between John the Baptist and Jesus, which was such a major topic in Luke 1 and 2, is taken up again in John's question to Jesus (7:18–23) and in Jesus' words about John (7:24–35). In light of 3:19–20, we are to assume that John is in prison, and thus unable to contact Jesus personally. The expression "he who is to come" may have been a messianic title derived from Psalm 118:26 and Malachi 3:1.

In answering the question of John's disciples, Jesus alludes to the list of deeds of the Messiah in Isaiah 35:5–6 and 61:1. There can be no doubt that Jesus is "the one he (John) said was going to come."

The departure of John's·messengers provides Jesus with the occasion to talk about John's identity and the significance of his rejection. Herod Antipas had John put in prison for questioning the propriety of his marriage to Herodias. Jesus contrasts John with other religious leaders of the time, and even with Herod, John's captor. John is greater than the other prophets, because he is the one promised in Malachi 3:1 and 4:5 who will precede the Messiah in Israel. According to 7:29–30, the public's response to John was mixed. In 7:31–35 Jesus compares those who show their skepticism to nasty children who refuse to play either the happy game of Jesus or the sad game of John.

The Messengers from John the Baptist
(Also Matt. 11.2–19)

[18]John's disciples told him about all these things. John called two of them to him [19]and sent them to the Lord to ask him, "Are you the one John said was going to come, or should we expect someone else?" [20]When they came to Jesus they said, "John the Baptist sent us to ask, 'Are you the one he said was going to come, or should we expect someone else?' " [21]At that very time Jesus healed many people from their sicknesses, diseases, and evil spirits, and gave sight to many blind people. [22]He answered John's messengers: "Go back and tell John what you have seen and heard: the blind can see, the lame can walk, the lepers are made clean, the deaf can hear, the dead are raised to life, and the Good News is preached to the poor. [23]How happy is he who has no doubts about me!"

[24]After John's messengers had left, Jesus began to speak about John to the crowds: "When you went out to John in the desert, what did you expect to see? A blade of grass bending in the wind? [25]What did you go out to see? A man dressed up in fancy clothes? Really, those who dress like that and live in luxury are found in palaces! [26]Tell me, what did you expect to see? A prophet? Yes, I tell you— you saw much more than a prophet. [27]For John is the one of whom the scripture says, 'Here is

my messenger, says God; I will send him ahead of you to open the way for you.' ²⁸I tell you," Jesus added, "John is greater than any man ever born; but he who is least in the Kingdom of God is greater than he."

²⁹All the people and the tax collectors heard him; they were the ones who had obeyed God's righteous demands and had been baptized by John. ³⁰But the Pharisees and the teachers of the Law rejected God's purpose for themselves, and refused to be baptized by John.

³¹Jesus continued, "Now, to what can I compare the people of this day? What are they like? ³²They are like children sitting in the marketplace. One group shouts to the other, 'We played wedding music for you, but you would not dance! We sang funeral songs, but you would not cry!' ³³John the Baptist came, and he fasted and drank no wine, and you said, 'He is a madman!' ³⁴The Son of Man came, and he ate and drank, and you said, 'Look at this man! He is a glutton and wine-drinker, and is a friend of tax collectors and outcasts!' ³⁵God's wisdom, however, is shown to be true by all who accept it."

The Sinful Woman

The criticism of Jesus for eating with tax collectors and sinners is taken up in the incident with the sinful woman at the Pharisee's banquet in 7:36–50. The incident occurs during a banquet held at the house of Simon the Pharisee. Communal meals with fellow Pharisees were very important social and religious occasions, and Jesus' practice of opening up his meals to people suspected of ritual uncleanness and sin would have been especially offensive to the Pharisees. Simon would not have dreamed of inviting such people to his house, though he was apparently curious enough about Jesus the teacher and healer to have invited him.

The story begins in 7:36–39 by drawing a contrast between the sinful woman and the Pharisee. The woman may have been a prostitute. Simon equates being a prophet with extraordinary knowledge. Jesus demonstrates this by revealing Simon's thoughts and commenting on them, rather than by rejecting the sinful woman. In 7:40–43 he explains the meaning of the incident to the Pharisee by means of a parable that at first seems to have no immediate application to the situation.

The third part of the story (7:44–46) returns to the contrast of characters begun in the first part. Who had behaved correctly—the sinful woman or the Pharisee? What criterion did Simon use in judging the woman? What criterion did Jesus the prophet use? The final part (7:47–50) goes back to the parable told in the second part. It emphasizes that love and forgiveness can never be separated.

The Women Disciples

The list of women who accompanied Jesus (8:1–3) follows the incident of the sinful woman and the Pharisee. There is, however, no reason to identify Mary Magdalene as the sinful woman. More important is the fact that Luke assumed that these women accompanied Jesus and the twelve apostles, and that the instructions on discipleship were intended for them also. It was most unusual that a Jewish teacher like Jesus would have been joined by a group of women disciples, and so we can be certain that the report rests on good historical foundations.

Jesus at the Home of Simon the Pharisee

³⁶A Pharisee invited Jesus to have dinner with him. Jesus went to his house and sat down to eat. ³⁷There was a woman in that town who lived a sinful life. She heard that Jesus was eating in the Pharisee's house, so she brought an alabaster jar full of perfume ³⁸and stood behind Jesus, by his feet, crying and wetting his feet with her tears. Then she dried his feet with her hair, kissed them, and poured the perfume on them. ³⁹When the Pharisee who had invited Jesus saw this, he said to himself, "If this man really were a prophet, he would know who this woman is who is touching him; he would know what kind of sinful life she leads!" ⁴⁰Jesus spoke up and said to him, "Simon, I have something to tell you." "Yes, Teacher," he said, "tell me." ⁴¹"There were two men who owed money to a moneylender," Jesus began. "One owed him five hundred dollars and the other one fifty dollars. ⁴²Neither one could pay him back, so he canceled the debts of both. Which one, then, will love him more?" ⁴³"I suppose," answered Simon, "that it would be the one who was forgiven more." "Your answer is correct," said Jesus. ⁴⁴Then he turned to the woman and said to Simon: "Do you see this woman? I came into your home, and you gave me no water for my feet, but she has washed my feet with her tears and dried them with her hair. ⁴⁵You did not welcome me with a kiss, but she has not stopped kissing my feet since I came. ⁴⁶You provided no oil for my head, but she has covered my feet with perfume. ⁴⁷I tell you, then, the great love she has shown proves that her many sins have been forgiven. Whoever has been forgiven little, however,

shows only a little love." [48]Then Jesus said to the woman, "Your sins are forgiven." [49]The others sitting at the table began to say to themselves, "Who is this, who even forgives sins?" [50]But Jesus said to the woman, "Your faith has saved you; go in peace."

Women Who Accompanied Jesus

8 Some time later Jesus made a trip through towns and villages, preaching the Good News about the Kingdom of God. The twelve disciples went with him, [2]and so did some women who had been healed of evil spirits and diseases: Mary (who was called Magdalene), from whom seven demons had been driven out; [3]Joanna, the wife of Chuza who was an officer in Herod's court; Susanna, and many other women who helped Jesus and his disciples with their belongings.

Revelation and Misunderstanding

The material in Luke 8:4—9:50 follows the outline set by Mark 4:1—6:44 and 8:27—9:41. Note that Mark 6:45—8:26 is omitted, a phenomenon sometimes described as Luke's "great omission." The central theme of this section of Luke's Gospel is revelation and misunderstanding. All kinds of people—religious rivals, political leaders, the crowds and even Jesus' own disciples—manage to misunderstand him despite the obvious power of his words and deeds. The growing misunderstanding will be resolved only by Jesus' instructions about himself and his disciples on the way up to Jerusalem in 9:51—19:44.

The parable of the sower in 8:4—8 explains why Jesus' preaching of God's kingdom was not universally accepted. The seed was good, but some kinds of soil were not receptive to it. Yet the seed that fell on the good soil yields a superabundant harvest. The mysterious and indirect style of his teaching (8:9–10) results in misunderstanding outside the circle of the disciples. This misunderstanding is similar to the experience described in Isaiah 6:9–10. Just as Isaiah the prophet was misunderstood, so Jesus the prophet is misunderstood. The explanation of the parable of the sower stresses the obstacles to interiorizing the Word of God and holds up as the model those who bring forth fruit with patience. The truth of Jesus' words (8:16–18) will shine like a lamp, even though many refuse it. The true family of Jesus is defined in 8:19–21 as those who hear the Word of God and do it. In the context of Luke's Gospel, Mary emerges as the ideal disciple.

The Parable of the Sower
(Also Matt. 13.1–9; Mark 4.1–9)

⁴People kept coming to Jesus from one town after another; and when a great crowd gathered, Jesus told this parable:

⁵"A man went out to sow his seed. As he scattered the seed in the field, some of it fell along the path, where it was stepped on, and the birds ate it. ⁶Some of it fell on rocky ground, and when the plants sprouted they dried up, because the soil had no moisture. ⁷Some of the seed fell among thorns which grew up with the plants and choked them. ⁸And some seeds fell in good soil; the plants grew and bore grain, one hundred grains each." And Jesus added, "Listen, then, if you have ears to hear with!"

⁹His disciples asked Jesus what this parable meant. ¹⁰Jesus answered, "The knowledge of the secrets of the Kingdom of God has

been given to you; but to the rest it comes by means of parables, so that they may look but not see, and listen but not understand."

Jesus Explains the Parable of the Sower
(Also Matt. 13.18—23; Mark 4.13—20)

[11]"This is what the parable means: the seed is the word of God. [12]The seed that fell along the path stands for those who hear; but the Devil comes and takes the message away from their hearts to keep them from believing and being saved. [13]The seed that fell on rocky ground stands for those who hear the message and receive it gladly. But it does not sink deep into them; they believe only for a while, and fall away when the time of temptation comes. [14]The seed that fell among thorns stands for those who hear; but the worries and riches and pleasures of this life crowd in and choke them, and their fruit never ripens. [15]The seed that fell in good soil stands for those who hear the message and retain it in a good and obedient heart, and persist until they bear fruit."

[16]"No one lights a lamp and covers it with a bowl or puts it under a bed. Instead, he puts it on the lamp-stand, so that people will see the light as they come in. [17]Whatever is hidden away will be brought out into the open, and whatever is covered up will be found and brought to light. [18]"Be careful, then, how you listen; for whoever has something will be given more, but whoever has nothing will have taken away from him even the little he thinks he has."

Jesus' Mother and Brothers
(Also Matt. 12.46–50; Mark 3.31–35)

¹⁹Jesus' mother and brothers came to him, but were unable to join him because of the crowd. ²⁰Someone said to Jesus, "Your mother and brothers are standing outside and want to see you." ²¹Jesus said to them all, "My mother and brothers are those who hear the word of God and obey it."

Jesus Calms a Storm
(Also Matt. 8.23–27; Mark 4.35–41)

²²One day Jesus got into a boat with his disciples and said to them, "Let us go across to the other side of the lake." So they started out. ²³As they were sailing, Jesus went to sleep. A strong wind blew down on the lake, and the boat began to fill with water, putting them all in great danger. ²⁴The disciples came to Jesus and woke him up, saying, "Master, Master! We are about to die!" Jesus got up and gave a command to the wind and to the stormy water; they quieted down and there was a great calm. ²⁵Then he said to the disciples, "Where is your faith?" But they were amazed and afraid, and said to one another: "Who is this man? He gives orders to the winds and waves, and they obey him!"

Miracles

Jesus' power over the sea, demons, diseases and even death as displayed in 8:22–56 makes the misunderstanding of him even more tragic. In stilling the storm at sea, Jesus responds to the disciples' plea, and displays a power attributed to God in several Old Testament passages (Psalm 74:13–17; 89:8–13; Isaiah

51:9–10; Job 38:8–11). In exorcising the demon from the man at Gerasa in 8:26–39, Jesus continues his task of breaking the power of Satan—a power explicitly rejected by the Son of God in the testing story (4:1–13). In curing the woman with the flow of blood and restoring Jairus' daughter to life in 8:40–56, Jesus appears as not merely a healer, but one who can give life.

Mission and Miraculous Feeding

In 9:1–6 the twelve apostles are sent forth to preach and heal as Jesus did. They must travel simply, for those who share in Jesus' authority must also share in his life-style. The account is interrupted by mention of Herod Antipas' puzzlement over Jesus and a reference to his execution of John the Baptist.

The return of the apostles leads into the story of the feeding of the 5,000 in 9:10–17. The language in which Jesus' actions are described ("[Jesus] looked up to heaven, thanked God for them, broke them and gave them to the disciples.") connects this miraculous feeding with the Last Supper and the other banquets so prominent in Luke's Gospel.

Jesus Heals a Man with Demons
(Also Matt. 8.28–34; Mark 4.1–20)

²⁶They sailed on over to the territory of the Gerasenes, which is across the lake from Galilee. ²⁷As Jesus stepped ashore, he was met by a man from the town who had demons in him. He had gone for a long time without clothes, and would not stay at home, but spent his time in the burial caves. ²⁸When he saw Jesus he gave a loud cry, fell down before him and said in a loud voice: "Jesus, Son of the Most High God! What do you want with me? I beg you, don't

punish me!" ²⁹He said this because Jesus had ordered the evil spirit to go out of him. Many times it had seized him, and even though he was kept a prisoner, his hands and feet tied with chains, he would break the chains and be driven by the demon out into the desert. ³⁰Jesus asked him, "What is your name?" "My name is 'Mob,'" he answered—because many demons had gone into him. ³¹The demons begged Jesus not to send them into the abyss.

³²A large herd of pigs was nearby, feeding on the hillside. The demons begged Jesus to let them go into the pigs—and he let them. ³³So the demons went out of the man and into the pigs; the whole herd rushed down the side of the cliff into the lake and were drowned.

³⁴The men who were taking care of the pigs saw what happened, so they ran off and spread the news in the town and among the farms. ³⁵People went out to see what had happened. They came to Jesus and found the man from whom the demons had gone out sitting at the feet of Jesus, clothed, and in his right mind— and they were all afraid. ³⁶Those who had seen it told the people how the man had been cured. ³⁷Then the whole crowd from the territory of the Gerasenes asked Jesus to go away, for they were all terribly afraid. So Jesus got into the boat and left. ³⁸The man from whom the demons had gone out begged Jesus, "Let me go with you." But Jesus sent him away, saying, ³⁹"Go back home and tell what God has done for you." The man went through the whole town telling what Jesus had done for him.

Jairus' Daughter and the Woman Who Touched Jesus' Cloak
(Also Matt. 9.18–26; Mark 5.21–43)

⁴⁰When Jesus returned to the other side of the lake the crowd welcomed him, for they had all been waiting for him. ⁴¹Then a man named Jairus arrived, an official in the local synagogue. He threw himself down at Jesus' feet and begged him to go to his home, ⁴²for his only daughter, twelve years old, was dying.

As Jesus went along, the people were crowding him from every side. ⁴³A certain woman was there who had suffered from severe bleeding for twelve years; she had spent all she had on doctors, but no one had been able to cure her. ⁴⁴She came up in the crowd behind Jesus and touched the edge of his cloak, and her bleeding stopped at once. ⁴⁵Jesus asked, "Who touched me?" Everyone denied it, and Peter said, "Master, the people are all around you and crowding in on you." ⁴⁶But Jesus said, "Someone touched me, for I knew it when power went out of me." ⁴⁷The woman saw that she had been found out, so she came, trembling, and threw herself at Jesus' feet. There, in front of everybody, she told him why she had touched him and how she had been healed at once. ⁴⁸Jesus said to her, "My daughter, your faith has made you well. Go in peace."

⁴⁹While Jesus was saying this, a messenger came from the official's house. "Your daughter has died," he told Jairus; "don't bother the Teacher any longer." ⁵⁰But Jesus heard it and said to Jairus, "Don't be afraid; only believe, and she will be well." ⁵¹When he arrived at the house he would not let anyone go in with him except Peter, John, and James, and the child's father and mother. ⁵²Everyone there was crying

and mourning for the child. Jesus said, "Don't cry; the child is not dead—she is only sleeping!" ⁵³They all made fun of him, because they knew that she was dead. ⁵⁴But Jesus took her by the hand and called out, "Get up, child!" ⁵⁵Her life returned and she got up at once; and Jesus ordered them to give her something to eat. ⁵⁶Her parents were astounded, but Jesus commanded them not to tell anyone what had happened.

Jesus Sends Out the Twelve Disciples
(Also Matt. 10.5—15; Mark 6.7—13)

9 Jesus called the twelve disciples together and gave them power and authority to drive out all demons and to cure diseases. ²Then he sent them out to preach the Kingdom of God and to heal the sick. ³He said to them: "Take nothing with you for the trip: no walking stick, no beggar's bag, no food, no money, not even an extra shirt. ⁴Wherever you are welcomed, stay in the same house until you leave that town; ⁵wherever people don't welcome you, leave that town and shake the dust off your feet as a warning to them." ⁶The disciples left and traveled through all the villages, preaching the Good News and healing people everywhere.

⁷Herod, the ruler of Galilee, heard about all the things that were happening; he was very confused about it because some people said, "John the Baptist has come back to life!" ⁸Others said that Elijah had appeared, while others said that one of the prophets of long ago had come back to life. ⁹Herod said, "I had John's head cut off; but who is this man I hear these things about?" And he kept trying to see Jesus.

Jesus Feeds Five Thousand
(Also Matt. 14.13–21; Mark 6.30–44; John 6.1–14)

¹⁰The apostles came back and told Jesus everything they had done. He took them with him and they went off by themselves to a town named Bethsaida. ¹¹When the crowds heard about it they followed him. He welcomed them, spoke to them about the Kingdom of God, and healed those who needed it.

¹²When the sun had begun to set, the twelve disciples came to him and said, "Send the people away so they can go to the villages and farms around here and find food and lodging; for this is a lonely place." ¹³But Jesus said to them, "You yourselves give them something to eat." They answered, "All we have is five loaves and two fish. Do you want us to go and buy food for this whole crowd?" ¹⁴(There were about five thousand men there.) Jesus said to his disciples, "Make the people sit down in groups of about fifty each." ¹⁵The disciples did so and made them all sit down. ¹⁶Jesus took the five loaves and two fish, looked up to heaven, thanked God for them, broke them, and gave them to the disciples to distribute to the people. ¹⁷They all ate and had enough; and the disciples took up twelve baskets of what was left over.

More Revelations and Misunderstandings

After the "great omission" of Mark 6:45–8:26, Luke signals the importance of what follows by telling us that Jesus was at prayer (9:18). Peter identifies Jesus as Messiah, the agent of God who will redeem Israel. Jesus accepts his confession of faith, but explains that suffering, death, and resurrection await him in Jerusalem. Just as the disciples shared in Jesus' power as a preacher and a healer, and in his simple life-style, so they must be ready to share in his suffering and death.

The account of the transfiguration in 9:28—36 establishes Jesus' identity as the Son of God before his teachings about himself and about discipleship on the road to Jerusalem in 9:51—19:44. The decisive importance of this event is emphasized by Luke's statement that Jesus went up to the mountain to pray and that the transfiguration took place while he was praying. As at the baptism, a connection is made between Jesus' prayer to his heavenly Father and the identification of Jesus as the Son of God. The disciples' inability to remain awake points forward to their behavior during Jesus' agony in the garden.

The remaining episodes in this section stress the disciples' misunderstanding of Jesus. Their failure to heal the boy with the unclean spirit in 9:37—43 places them among the faithless and perverse generation, and the plain meaning of Jesus' second passion prediction in 9:44—45 escapes them entirely. Their arguing about who is the greatest reveals that they have not yet grasped what Jesus is all about. Their narrowness in trying to stop the unknown exorcist in 9:49—50 shows how much they need solid instruction about Jesus and their relation to him. That instruction is provided on the long journey to Jerusalem.

■ Reflection
Am I willing to accept all of Jesus' preaching and act on it?

Peter's Declaration About Jesus
(Also Matt. 16.13–19; Mark 3.27–29)

¹⁸One time when Jesus was praying alone, the disciples came to him. "Who do the crowds say I am?" he asked them. ¹⁹"Some say that you are John the Baptist," they answered. "Others say that you are Elijah, while others say that one of the prophets of long ago has come back to life." ²⁰"What about you?" he asked them. "Who do you say I am?" Peter answered, "You are God's Messiah!"

²¹Then Jesus gave them strict orders not to tell this to anyone, ²²and added: "The Son of Man must suffer much, and be rejected by the elders, the chief priests, and the teachers of the Law. He will be put to death, and be raised to life on the third day."

²³And he said to all: "If anyone wants to come with me, he must forget himself, take up his cross every day, and follow me. ²⁴For the person who wants to save his own life will lose it; but the one who loses his life for my sake will save it. ²⁵Will a man gain anything if he wins the whole world but is himself lost or defeated? Of course not! ²⁶If a man is ashamed of me and of my teaching, then the Son of Man will be ashamed of him when he comes in his glory and the glory of the Father and of the holy angels. ²⁷Remember this! There are some here, I tell you, who will not die until they have seen the Kingdom of God."

²⁸About a week after he had said these things, Jesus took Peter, John, and James with him and went up a hill to pray. ²⁹While he was praying, his face changed its appearance and his clothes became dazzling white. ³⁰Suddenly two men were there talking with him. They

were Moses and Elijah, ³¹who appeared in heavenly glory and talked with Jesus about how he would soon fulfill God's purpose by dying in Jerusalem. ³²Peter and his companions were sound asleep, but they awoke and saw Jesus' glory and the two men who were standing with him. ³³As the men were leaving Jesus, Peter said to him: "Master, it is a good thing that we are here. We will make three tents, one for you, one for Moses, and one for Elijah." (He really did not know what he was saying.) ³⁴While he was still speaking, a cloud appeared and covered them with its shadow, and the disciples were afraid as the cloud came over them. ³⁵A voice said from the cloud: "This is my Son, whom I have chosen—listen to him!" ³⁶When the voice stopped, there was Jesus all alone. The disciples kept quiet about all this, and told no one at that time a single thing they had seen.

Jesus Heals a Boy with an Evil Spirit
(Also Matt. 17.14—18; Mark 9.14—27)

³⁷The next day they went down from the hill, and a large crowd met Jesus. ³⁸A man shouted from the crowd: "Teacher! Look, I beg you, at my son—my only son! ³⁹A spirit attacks him with a sudden shout and throws him into a fit, so that he foams at the mouth; it keeps on hurting him and will hardly let him go! ⁴⁰I begged your disciples to drive it out, but they could not." ⁴¹Jesus answered: "How unbelieving and wrong you people are! How long must I stay with you? How long do I have to put up with you?" Then he said to the man, "Bring your son here." ⁴²As the boy was coming, the demon knocked him to the ground and threw him into a fit. Jesus gave a command to the

evil spirit, healed the boy, and gave him back to his father. [43]All the people were amazed at the mighty power of God.

The people were still marveling at everything Jesus was doing, when he said to his disciples: [44]"Don't forget what I am about to tell you! The Son of Man is going to be handed over to the power of men." [45]But they did not know what this meant. It had been hidden from them so that they could not understand it, and they were afraid to ask him about the matter.

Who Is the Greatest?
(Also Matt. 18.1–4; Mark 9.33–37)

[46]An argument came up among the disciples as to which one of them was the greatest. [47]Jesus knew what they were thinking, so he took a child, stood him by his side, [48]and said to them: "The person who in my name welcomes this child, welcomes me; and whoever welcomes me, also welcomes the one who sent me. For he who is least among you all is the greatest."

Who Is Not Against You Is For You
(Also Mark 9.38–40)

[49]John spoke up. "Master," he said, "we saw a man driving out demons in your name, and we told him to stop, because he doesn't belong to our group." [50]"Do not try to stop him," Jesus said to him and to the other disciples; "for whoever is not against you is for you."

■ *Reflection*

If Jesus were beginning his ministry in the 1980s, with what kinds of people would he associate?

■ Discussion

1. Are Jesus' moral teachings in the Sermon on the Plain reasonable in terms of contemporary values and needs?

2. What kinds of people are the objects of Jesus' concern? What are their attitudes toward him?

3. How would you describe the relation between Jesus and John the Baptist?

4. Why was Jesus' preaching not universally accepted?

5. What insights into the celebration of the Eucharist can we gain from the story of the feeding of the 5,000?

■ Prayer and Meditation

"Before I was born, the LORD appointed me;
> he made me his servant to bring back his people,
> to bring back the scattered people of Israel.

The LORD gives me honor;
> he is the source of my strength.

The LORD said to me,

'I have a greater task for you, my servant.
> Not only will you restore to greatness
> the people of Israel who have survived,

but I will also make you a light to the nations—
> so that all the world may be saved.' "

Isaiah 49:5–6

The Journey Begins/and Continues —— Luke 9:51—13:30

The central section of Luke's Gospel (9:51—19:44) tells the story of the journey of Jesus and his disciples from Galilee to Jerusalem. Although the idea of a final journey was present in Mark 8:22—10:52, Luke expanded the journey greatly and made it the vehicle for including many of Jesus' teachings. The two major themes are Christology (who Jesus is) and discipleship (who his followers are in relation to him).

Jesus freely accepts this journey toward suffering, for through it he will enter into glory. Along the way he teaches the disciples and us about the kingdom of God, the resurrection, and the second coming. He also spells out themes of great importance for all who wish to be his followers: the cost of discipleship, the universal character of salvation, forgiveness of sins, receptivity to revelation, love of God and neighbor, sharing wealth, and rejoicing over the conversion of sinners.

The journey is tied in from the very beginning to its eventual goal, the events of the passion, death, resurrection, and ascension. Jesus plans for his journey and the activities along the way by sending out messengers to prepare for his arrival at different places along the journey.

Rejection and Discipleship

From the very beginning, Jesus is misunderstood. First he is misunderstood by the Samaritans (9:52–53). They see him as choosing the Jewish community over their own concerns, because he is journeying to Jerusalem, the center of Jewish worship and culture. They wish to involve him in the Jewish/Samaritan controversy over who are the true followers of Moses, the true people of God.

Next he is misunderstood by his own disciples (9:54–56). Having heard Jesus' discourse on loving one's enemies in the Sermon on the Plain, Jesus' disciples are unable to apply this principle of the new order which Jesus is about to establish. They expect him to act like Elijah in 2 Kings 1:9–12, destroying his enemies in a dramatic way, a scenario out of the Old Testament, not the new law of the kingdom of God.

The progress of the journey is the occasion for teachings about the demands of discipleship (9:57–62). These demands are harsh. In some cases they involve disregard of physical security and family obligations. They are based on the example of Jesus himself. His teachings in this section should not be taken as attacks on the family and devotion to it, but rather as extreme ways of emphasizing the ultimate importance of proclaiming the Gospel.

■ Reflection

What misunderstandings about Jesus and his mission are common among Christians today?

A Samaritan Village Refuses to Receive Jesus

⁵¹As the days drew near when Jesus would be taken up to heaven, he made up his mind and set out on his way to Jerusalem. ⁵²He sent messengers ahead of him, who left and went into a Samaritan village to get everything ready for him. ⁵³But the people there would not receive him, because it was plain that he was going to Jerusalem. ⁵⁴When the disciples James and John saw this they said, "Lord, do you want us to call fire down from heaven and destroy them?" ⁵⁵Jesus turned and rebuked them; ⁵⁶and they went on to another village.

⁵⁷As they went on their way, a certain man said to Jesus, "I will follow you wherever you go." ⁵⁸Jesus said to him, "Foxes have holes, and birds have nests, but the Son of Man has no place to lie down and rest." ⁵⁹He said to another man, "Follow me." But he said, "Sir, first let me go and bury my father." ⁶⁰Jesus answered, "Let the dead bury their own dead. You go and preach the Kingdom of God." ⁶¹Another man said, "I will follow you, sir; but first let me go and say good-bye to my family." ⁶²Jesus said to him, "Anyone who starts to plow and then keeps looking back is of no use for the Kingdom of God."

The Mission of the Seventy Disciples

In 10:1–6, Jesus sends out seventy disciples on a mission. His instructions reflect his own life as a traveling preacher, and would have challenged the early apostles who continued Jesus' mission to act in the same way. The Mediterranean world of Luke's time was fully accustomed to wandering preachers of various religions and philosophies, and so Jesus' instructions would have served as a checklist for people to distinguish the genuine missionaries from the imposters.

The second part of the instruction (10:5–9) describes how the missionaries are to behave when they stop in a town. The traditional Jewish way of saying "hello" is "peace" *(shalom)*. It includes all the blessings and good things anyone could wish for another person. In this context a "peace-loving man" (10:6) would be anyone open to the message of the kingdom.

The disciples who did not know how to handle rejection by the Samaritan villagers in 9:54–56 are given instruction in 10:10–12 on how to deal with rejection. The disciples can expect rejection in certain cities, since Jesus himself experienced it. Corazin and Bethsaida were cities in Galilee, while Tyre and Sidon were pagan cities in Phoenicia frequently denounced in the Old Testament.

The mission of the seventy was a great success, and they returned with joy in their hearts (10:17). While sharing their joy, Jesus places their mission in its proper perspective in 10:18–24. His vision of Satan's fall from heaven is based on the Old Testament idea that Satan was a member of the heavenly court (see Job 1–2; Zechariah 3:1–5). Now Satan has been ejected from the heavenly court, and on earth his power is being broken by Jesus and those who share in Jesus' power. The disciples' power over demons is part of the larger triumph of Jesus over Satan.

The importance of the event is marked by prayer. In this case, Luke not only mentions that Jesus prayed, but tells us the content of the prayer. The relationship between the Father, Jesus, and the disciples which is alluded to in 10:16, is made clear in the context of revelation.

Jesus Sends Out the Seventy-two

10 After this the Lord chose another seventy-two men and sent them out, two by two, to go ahead of him to every town and place where he himself was about to go. ²He said to them: "There is a great harvest, but few workers to gather it in. Pray to the owner of the harvest that he will send out more workers to gather in his harvest. ³Go! I am sending you like lambs among wolves. ⁴Don't take a purse, or a beggar's bag, or shoes; don't stop to greet anyone on the road. ⁵Whenever you go into a house, first say, 'Peace be with this house.' ⁶If a peace-loving man lives there, let your greeting of peace remain on him; if not, take back your greeting of peace. ⁷Stay in that same house, eating and drinking what they offer you; for a worker should be given his pay. Don't move around from one house to another. ⁸Whenever you go into a town and are made welcome, eat what is set before you, ⁹heal the sick in that town, and say to the people there, 'The Kingdom of God has come near you.' ¹⁰But whenever you go into a town and are not welcomed there, go out in the streets and say, ¹¹'Even the dust from your town that sticks to our feet we wipe off against you; but remember this, the Kingdom of God has come near you!' ¹²I tell you that on the Judgment Day God will show more mercy to Sodom than to that town!''

¹³''How terrible it will be for you, Chorazin! How terrible for you too, Bethsaida! For if the miracles which were performed in you had been performed in Tyre and Sidon long ago, the people there would have sat down, put on sackcloth, and sprinkled ashes on themselves to show that they had turned from their sins! ¹⁴God will show more mercy on the Judgment Day to

Tyre and Sidon than to you. ¹⁵And as for you, Capernaum! You wanted to lift yourself up to heaven? You will be thrown down to hell!''

¹⁶He said to his disciples: "Whoever listens to you, listens to me; whoever rejects you, rejects me; and whoever rejects me, rejects the one who sent me.''

The Return of the Seventy-two

¹⁷The seventy-two men came back in great joy. "Lord,'' they said, "even the demons obeyed us when we commanded them in your name!'' ¹⁸Jesus answered them: "I saw Satan fall like lightning from heaven. ¹⁹Listen! I have given you authority, so that you can walk on snakes and scorpions, and over all the power of the Enemy, and nothing will hurt you. ²⁰But don't be glad because the evil spirits obey you; rather be glad because your names are written in heaven.''

²¹At that same time Jesus was filled with joy by the Holy Spirit, and said: "O Father, Lord of heaven and earth! I thank you because you have shown to the unlearned what you have hidden from the wise and learned. Yes, Father, this was done by your own choice and pleasure.

²²"My Father has given me all things: no one knows who the Son is except the Father, and no one knows who the Father is except the Son and those to whom the Son wants to reveal him.''

²³Then Jesus turned to the disciples and said to them privately: "How happy are you, to see the things you see! ²⁴For many prophets and kings, I tell you, wanted to see what you see,

but they could not, and to hear what you hear,
but they did not."

Love of God and Neighbor

Jesus and his disciples have been on a journey from Galilee to Jerusalem since 9:51. Having sent the seventy disciples on a mission and having placed that mission in a proper context, Jesus now teaches about love of neighbor in the parable of the good Samaritan, and about love of God in the instruction on prayer. The story of Martha and Mary (10:38–42) concerns the balance between love of neighbor and love of God. Serving the neighbor is very important, but not quite as important as serving God.

The occasion for these teachings is provided by a dialogue between Jesus and a lawyer (10:25–28). The law in which the lawyer was an expert was the Old Testament and the regulations deduced from it. Jewish teachers of Jesus' time were often asked to summarize the law by means of a brief statement and so the lawyer's question to Jesus was not unusual or perhaps even unexpected.

The lawyer's defensive question about who is his neighbor is answered by the parable of the good Samaritan. The main character is the man who was robbed. The road from Jerusalem to Jericho descends through a mountainous area and was well known as a haunt for robbers.

The theme of the story told by Jesus is the law vs. love, or the meaning of the law. The priest and the Levite may have avoided the stranger on the road because they thought he was either dead or diseased. By touching him, they would have become ritually unclean and, therefore, unable to take part in public worship.

The Samaritan is the surprise hero, since the animosity between Samaritans and Jews was an expected attitude. Neither associated with the other because of religious differences. But Jesus demonstrates through the story that love is more important than religious law or religious bigotry.

■ *Reflection*

If we are in real trouble, do we refuse help from anyone? Do we respond to those in need on the basis of what society expects or on the basis of what love requires?

The Parable of the Good Samaritan

²⁵Then a certain teacher of the Law came up and tried to trap Jesus. "Teacher," he asked, "what must I do to receive eternal life?" ²⁶Jesus answered him, "What do the Scriptures say? How do you interpret them?" ²⁷The man answered: " 'You must love the Lord your God with all your heart, and with all your soul, and with all your strength, and with all your mind'; and, 'You must love your neighbor as yourself.' " ²⁸"Your answer is correct," replied Jesus; "do this and you will live."

²⁹But the teacher of the Law wanted to put himself in the right, so he asked Jesus, "Who is my neighbor?" ³⁰Jesus answered: "A certain man was going down from Jerusalem to Jericho, when robbers attacked him, stripped him and beat him up, leaving him half dead. ³¹It so happened that a priest was going down that road; when he saw the man he walked on

by, on the other side. ³²In the same way a Levite also came there, went over and looked at the man, and then walked on by, on the other side. ³³But a certain Samaritan who was traveling that way came upon him, and when he saw the man his heart was filled with pity. ³⁴He went over to him, poured oil and wine on his wounds and bandaged them; then he put the man on his own animal and took him to an inn, where he took care of him. ³⁵The next day he took out two silver coins and gave them to the innkeeper.'Take care of him,' he told the innkeeper, 'and when I come back this way I will pay you back whatever you spend on him.' " ³⁶And Jesus concluded, "Which one of these three seems to you to have been a neighbor to the man attacked by the robbers?" ³⁷The teacher of the Law answered, "The one who was kind to him." Jesus replied, "You go, then, and do the same."

As Jesus continues on the way to Jerusalem, he is offered hospitality by a woman named Martha (10:38–42). In a culture in which women did not normally share in intellectual discussion, Jesus' insistence that Mary and Martha be allowed to listen to his teaching would have been surprising.

The Gospel of Luke is sometimes called the Gospel of prayer, because in it Jesus prays at the decisive points of his life, and gives instructions on prayer not found elsewhere in the Gospels. In the context of Jesus' journey to Jerusalem, his teaching on prayer in 11:1–13 shows how we are to express our love for God. It consists of a sample prayer (11:1–4), a story stressing persistence in prayer (11:5–8), and sayings emphasizing God's eagerness to hear our prayers (11:9–13).

In response to the disciples' request for instruction on how to pray, Jesus teaches them the Lord's Prayer. The version of the Our Father in Matthew 6:9–13 is used most commonly in the Church, but some features in Luke's version may reflect Jesus' original wording.

The importance of persistence in prayer of petition is illustrated by the parable of the friend at midnight in 11:5–8. This theme occurs again in the parables of the unjust judge and the persistent widow in 18:1–8. Prayer is the proper avenue for gaining favor with God. He is eager to hear our prayers (11:9–13), but we must be persistent in bringing our needs to him.

Jesus Visits Martha and Mary

[38]As Jesus and his disciples went on their way, he came to a certain village where a woman named Martha welcomed him in her home. [39]She had a sister named Mary, who sat down at the feet of the Lord and listened to his teaching. [40]Martha was upset over all the work she had to do; so she came and said, "Lord, don't you care that my sister has left me to do all the work by myself? Tell her to come and help me!" [41]The Lord answered her, "Martha, Martha! You are worried and troubled over so many things, [42]but just one is needed. Mary has chosen the right thing, and it will not be taken away from her."

Jesus' Teaching on Prayer
(Also Matt. 6.9–13; 7.7–11)

11 One time Jesus was praying in a certain place. When he finished, one of his disciples said to him, "Lord, teach us to pray, just as John taught his disciples." [2]Jesus said

to them, "This is what you should pray:
'Father,
May your name be kept holy,
May your Kingdom come.
³Give us day by day the food we need.
⁴Forgive us our sins,
For we forgive everyone who has done us wrong.
And do not bring us to hard testing.' "

⁵And Jesus said to his disciple: "Suppose one of you should go to a friend's house at midnight and tell him, 'Friend, let me borrow three loaves of bread. ⁶A friend of mine who is on a trip has just come to my house and I don't have a thing to offer him!' ⁷And suppose your friend should answer from inside, 'Don't bother me! The door is already locked, my children and I are in bed, and I can't get up to give you anything.' ⁸Well, what then? I tell you, even if he will not get up and give you the bread because he is your friend, yet he will get up and give you everything you need because you are not ashamed to keep on asking. ⁹And so I say to you: Ask, and you will receive; seek, and you will find; knock, and the door will be opened to you. ¹⁰For everyone who asks will receive, and he who seeks will find, and the door will be opened to him who knocks. ¹¹Would any one of you fathers give his son a snake when he asks for fish? ¹²Or would you give him a scorpion when he asks for an egg? ¹³As bad as you are, you know how to give good things to your children. How much more, then, the Father in heaven will give the Holy Spirit to those who ask him!"

Teachings on the Kingdom—
A Bridge

As Jesus and the disciples continue their journey through Galilee in 11:14—13:30, the total commitment to the kingdom of God that is demanded of Jesus' followers is brought into focus. The healing of a possessed man who was mute (11:14) furnishes the occasion for Jesus to make clear that his power is not from Satan, that his exorcisms are anticipations of God's kingdom, and that he has power over the chief demon (11:17–23). That power was already proved in the testing story (4:1–13). However, the power of the evil spirits has not been broken entirely (11:24–26). In fact, the passion story will begin with the reappearance of Satan and his entrance into Judas (see 22:3). The true follower of Jesus (11:27–28) hears the Word of God and keeps it. As was the case in 8:19–21, Mary the mother of Jesus emerges from this definition as the ideal disciple.

The sign for this generation is the sign of Jonah—the preaching of repentance to non-Jews such as the people of Nineveh and the Queen of Sheba (see 1 Kings 10:1–6), and its acceptance by them. Even though this sign is as clear as a lamp in the darkness (11:33), the opponents of Jesus fail to see it because they lack spiritual vision (11:34–36).

Jesus and Beelzebul
(Also Matt. 12.22–30; Mark 3.20–27)

[14]Jesus was driving out a demon that could not talk; when the demon went out, the man began to talk. The crowds were amazed, [15]but some of them said, "It is Beelzebul, the chief of the demons, who gives him the power to drive them out." [16]Others wanted to trap him, so they

asked him to perform a miracle to show God's approval. ¹⁷But Jesus knew their thoughts and said to them: "Any country that divides itself into groups that fight one another will not last very long; a family divided against itself falls apart. ¹⁸So if Satan's kingdom has groups fighting each other, how can it last? You say that I drive out demons because Beelzebul gives me the power to do so. ¹⁹If this is how I drive them out, how do your followers drive them out? Your own followers prove that you are completely wrong! ²⁰No, it is rather by means of God's power that I drive out demons, which proves that the Kingdom of God has already come to you.

²¹"When a strong man, with all his weapons ready, guards his own house, all his belongings are safe. ²²But when a stronger man attacks him and defeats him, he carries away all the weapons the owner was depending on and divides up what he stole.

²³"Anyone who is not for me, is really against me; anyone who does not help me gather, is really scattering."

The Return of the Evil Spirit
(Also Matt. 12.43—45)

²⁴"When an evil spirit goes out of a man, it travels over dry country looking for a place to rest; if it doesn't find one, it says to itself, 'I will go back to my house which I left.' ²⁵So it goes back and finds the house clean and all fixed up. ²⁶Then it goes out and brings seven other spirits even worse than itself, and they come and live there. So that man is in worse shape, when it is all over, than he was at the beginning."

²⁷When Jesus had said this, a woman spoke up from the crowd and said to him, "How happy is the woman who bore you and nursed you!" ²⁸But Jesus answered, "Rather, how happy are those who hear the word of God and obey it!"

The Demand for a Miracle
(Also Matt. 12.38—42)

²⁹As the people crowded around Jesus he went on to say: "How evil are the people of this day! They ask for a miracle as a sign of God's approval, but none will be given them except the miracle of Jonah. ³⁰In the same way that the prophet Jonah was a sign for the people of Nineveh, so the Son of Man will be a sign for the people of this day. ³¹On the Judgment Day the Queen from the South will stand up and accuse the people of today, because she traveled halfway around the world to listen to Solomon's wise teaching; and there is something here, I tell you, greater than Solomon. ³²On the Judgment Day the people of Nineveh will stand up and accuse you, because they turned from their sins when they heard Jonah preach; and there is something here, I tell you, greater than Jonah!"

The Light of the Body
(Also Matt. 5.15; 6.22—23)

³³"No one lights a lamp and then hides it or puts it under a bowl; instead, he puts it on the lamp-stand, so that people may see the light as they come in. ³⁴Your eyes are like a lamp for the body: when your eyes are clear your whole body is full of light; but when your eyes are bad

your whole body will be in darkness. ³⁵Be careful, then, that the light in you is not darkness. ³⁶If, then, your whole body is full of light, with no part of it in darkness, it will be bright all over, as when a lamp shines on you with its brightness.''

True and False Spiritualities

A meal at the house of a Pharisee is the occasion for Jesus to distinguish the false spirituality of the Pharisees and the lawyers from the true spirituality of his followers (11:37–52). The thrust of Jesus' critique of the Pharisees is that they are more concerned with external matters than with genuine spirituality. By his woes pronounced against the Pharisees, Jesus suggests that true spirituality focuses on justice and love of God, avoids public display for its own sake, and is alive inside. By his woes pronounced against the lawyers, Jesus insists that true spiritual leaders do not burden people, do not kill prophets and apostles, and do not close up knowledge.

Fearless Confession

Having been warned against the hypocrisy of the Pharisees (12:1), the disciples are encouraged to be fearless in their profession of faith because their opponents will be exposed at the last judgment and they will be vindicated (12:2–9). The only unforgivable sin is to attribute to an evil spirit what is the work of the Holy Spirit. The same Holy Spirit will remain faithful to faithful Christians (12:11–12).

Jesus Accuses the Pharisees and the Teachers of the Law
(Also Matt. 23.1–36; Mark 12.38–40)

[37]When Jesus finished speaking, a Pharisee invited him to eat with him; so he went in and sat down to eat. [38]The Pharisee was surprised when he noticed that Jesus had not washed before eating. [39]So the Lord said to him: "Now, then, you Pharisees clean the cup and plate on the outside, but inside you are full of violence and evil. [40]Fools! Did not God, who made the outside, also make the inside? [41]But give what is in your cups and plates to the poor, and everything will be clean for you.

[42]"How terrible for you, Pharisees! You give to God one tenth of the seasoning herbs, such as mint and rue and all the other herbs, but you neglect justice and the love for God. These you should practice, without neglecting the others.

[43]"How terrible for you, Pharisees! You love the reserved seats in the synagogues, and to be greeted with respect in the market places. [44]How terrible for you! You are like unmarked graves which people walk on without knowing it."

[45]One of the teachers of the Law said to him, "Teacher, when you say this you insult us too!" [46]Jesus answered: "How terrible for you, too, teachers of the Law! You put loads on men's backs which are hard to carry, but you yourselves will not stretch out a finger to help them carry those loads. [47]How terrible for you! You make fine tombs for the prophets—the very prophets your ancestors murdered. [48]You yourselves admit, then, that you approve of what your ancestors did; for they murdered the

prophets, and you build their tombs. [49]For this reason the Wisdom of God said: 'I will send them prophets and messengers; they will kill some of them and persecute others.' [50]So the people of this time will be punished for the murder of all the prophets killed since the creation of the world, [51]from the murder of Abel to the murder of Zechariah, who was killed between the altar and the holy place. Yes, I tell you, the people of this time will be punished for them all!

[52]"How terrible for you, teachers of the Law! You have kept the key that opens the door to the house of knowledge, you yourselves will not go in, and you stop those who are trying to go in!"

[53]When Jesus left that place the teachers of the Law and the Pharisees began to criticize him bitterly and ask him questions about many things, [54]trying to lay traps for him and catch him in something wrong he might say.

A Warning Against Hypocrisy
(Also Matt. 10.26–27)

12 As thousands of people crowded together, so that they were stepping on each other, Jesus said first to his disciples: "Be on guard against the yeast of the Pharisees—I mean their hypocrisy. [2]Whatever is covered up will be uncovered, and every secret will be made known. [3]So then, whatever you have said in the dark will be heard in broad daylight, and whatever you have whispered in men's ears in a closed room will be shouted from the housetops."

⁴"I tell you, my friends, do not be afraid of those who kill the body but cannot afterward do anything worse. ⁵I will show you whom to fear: fear God who, after killing, has the authority to throw into hell. Yes, I tell you, be afraid of him!

⁶"Aren't five sparrows sold for two pennies? Yet not a single one of them is forgotten by God. ⁷Even the hairs of your head have all been numbered. So do not be afraid: you are worth much more than many sparrows!"

Confessing and Rejecting Christ
(Also Matt. 10.32–33; 12.32; 10.19–20)

⁸"I tell you: whoever declares publicly that he belongs to me, the Son of Man will do the same for him before the angels of God; ⁹but whoever denies publicly that he belongs to me, the Son of Man will also deny him before the angels of God.

¹⁰"Anyone who says a word against the Son of Man will be forgiven; but the one who says evil things against the Holy Spirit will not be forgiven.

¹¹"When they bring you to be tried in the synagogues, or before governors or rulers, do not be worried about how you will defend yourself or what you will say. ¹²For the Holy Spirit will teach you at that time what you should say."

Material Concerns

The parable of the rich fool (12:13–21) stresses that one's relationship to God, not material wealth, is the most important thing in life. Jesus uses the occasion of being asked to decide an inheritance case to talk about what is truly important in life. To illustrate his point, he uses the story of a rich landowner to show that whoever makes material wealth into the key to happiness is a fool. The sayings on care and anxiety in 12:22–34 seek to liberate Jesus' followers from excessive concern about material wealth. If the heart is set on God, material things will take care of themselves.

Watchfulness

The master-servant parables in 12:35–48 illustrate what kind of attitude the disciples of Jesus should have toward the future coming of the Son of Man. The key word is watchfulness or vigilance. The servant must always be ready to light the master's way whenever he may come. The master will reward the servant's watchfulness, especially if he comes at a late hour. Since the precise time of the master's arrival is not known, you should always be on guard. Blessed are those servants who are found doing what they are supposed to be doing. The master's delay must not be used as an excuse for inappropriate action. The judgment will be particularly hard on those who knew their obligations, but failed to carry them out.

The Parable of the Rich Fool

[13]A man in the crowd said to him, "Teacher, tell my brother to divide with me the property our father left us." [14]Jesus answered him, "Man, who gave me the right to judge, or to divide the property beween you two?" [15]And he went on to say to them all: "Watch out, and guard yourselves from all kinds of greed; for a man's true life is not made up of the things he owns, no matter how rich he may be." [16]Then

Jesus told them this parable: "A rich man had land which bore good crops. ¹⁷He began to think to himself, 'I don't have a place to keep all my crops. What can I do? ¹⁸This is what I will do,' he told himself; 'I will tear my barns down and build bigger ones, where I will store the grain and all my other goods. ¹⁹Then I will say to myself: Lucky man! You have all the good things you need for many years. Take life easy, eat, drink, and enjoy yourself!' ²⁰But God said to him, 'You fool! This very night you will have to give up your life; then who will get all these things you have kept for yourself?' " ²¹And Jesus concluded, "This is how it is with those who pile up riches for themselves but are not rich in God's sight."

Trust in God
(Also Matt. 6.25–34)

²²Then Jesus said to the disciples: "This is why I tell you: Do not be worried about the food you need to stay alive, or about the clothes you need for your body. ²³For life is much more important than food, and the body much more important than clothes. ²⁴Look at the crows: they don't plant seeds or gather a harvest; they don't have storage rooms or barns; God feeds them! You are worth so much more than birds! ²⁵Which one of you can live a few more years by worrying about it? ²⁶If you can't manage even such a small thing, why worry about the other things? ²⁷Look how the wild flowers grow: they don't work or make clothes for themselves. But I tell you that not even Solomon, as rich as he was, had clothes as beautiful as one of these flowers. ²⁸It is God who clothes the wild grass— grass that is here today, gone tomorrow, burned up in the oven. Won't he be all the more

sure to clothe you? How little is your faith! [29]So don't be all upset, always looking for what you will eat and drink. [30](For the heathens of this world are always looking for all these things.) Your Father knows that you need these things. [31]Instead, put his Kingdom first in your life, and he will provide you with these things."

Riches in Heaven
(Also Matt. 6.19–21)

[32]"Do not be afraid, little flock! For your Father is pleased to give you the Kingdom. [33]Sell all your belongings and give the money to the poor. Provide for yourselves purses that don't wear out, and save your riches in heaven, where they will never decrease, for no thief can get to them, no moth can destroy them. [34]For your heart will always be where your riches are."

Watchful Servants

[35]"Be ready for whatever comes, with your clothes fastened tight at the waist and your lamps lit, [36]like servants who are waiting for their master to come back from a wedding feast. When he comes and knocks, they will open the door for him at once. [37]How happy are those servants whose master finds them awake and ready! I tell you, he will fasten his belt, have them sit down, and wait on them. [38]How happy are they if he finds them ready, even if he should come as late as midnight or even later! [39]And remember this! If the man of the house knew the time when the thief would come, he would not let the thief break into his house. [40]And you, too, be ready, because the

Son of Man will come at an hour when you are not expecting him."

⁴¹Peter said, "Lord, are you telling this parable to us, or do you mean it for everybody?" ⁴²The Lord answered: "Who, then, is the faithful and wise servant? He is the one whom his master will put in charge, to run the household and give the other servants their share of the food at the proper time. ⁴³How happy is that servant if his master finds him doing this when he comes home! ⁴⁴Indeed, I tell you, the master will put that servant in charge of all his property. ⁴⁵But if that servant says to himself, 'My master is taking a long time to come back,' and begins to beat the other servants, both men and women, and eats and drinks and gets drunk, ⁴⁶then the master will come back some day when the servant does not expect him and at a time he does not know; the master will cut him to pieces, and make him share the fate of the disobedient.

⁴⁷"The servant who knows what his master wants him to do, but does not get himself ready and do what his master wants, will be punished with a heavy whipping; ⁴⁸but the servant who does not know what his master wants, and does something for which he deserves a whipping, will be punished with a light whipping. The man to whom much is given, of him much is required; the man to whom more is given, of him much more is required."

Admission to God's Kingdom

The present time will involve the disciples in a baptism of suffering (12:49–50), and Jesus puts before them the extreme case of conflict within the family (12:51–53). It is necessary to discern the signs of the times (12:54–56) and to act shrewdly and decisively (12:57–59). The need for quick and decisive repentance is illustrated by references to some Galileans who had been executed and some Judeans who had been killed in an accident (13:1–5). This is balanced by the parable of the vinedresser in which the patience of God in awaiting our repentance is emphasized (13:6–9).

The healing of a crippled woman on the Sabbath (13:10–17) focuses attention again on the power of Jesus and his authority over the Old Testament law and Satan (13:16). The parables of the mustard seed and the leaven (13:18–21) suggest that, even though God's activity in Jesus seems very small, its result in the fullness of God's rule will be great. Admission to the heavenly banquet in God's kingdom (13:22–30) is not automatic or guaranteed to those who are Jewish by birth. Indeed some Jews will find themselves excluded from the banquet, while many non-Jews will share the feast with the great figures of Israel's religious tradition.

■ *Reflection*

How can contemporary Christians practice vigilance? Is it really necessary?

Jesus, the Cause of Division
(Also Matt. 10.34–36)

[49]"I came to set the earth on fire, and how I wish it were already kindled! [50]I have a baptism to receive, and how distressed I am until it is over! [51]Do you suppose that I came to bring peace to the world? Not peace, I tell you, but division. [52]From now on a family of five will be divided, three against two, two against three. [53]Fathers will be against their sons, and sons against their fathers; mothers will be against their daughters,

and daughters against their mothers; mothers-in-law will be against their daughters-in-law, and daughters-in-law against their mothers-in-law."

⁵⁴Jesus said also to the people: "When you see a cloud coming up in the west, at once you say, 'It is going to rain,' and it does. ⁵⁵And when you feel the south wind blowing, you say, 'It is going to get hot,' and it does. ⁵⁶Impostors! You can look at the earth and the sky and tell what it means; why, then, don't you know the meaning of this present time?"

⁵⁷"And why do you not judge for yourselves the right things to do? ⁵⁸If a man brings a lawsuit against you and takes you to court, do your best to settle the matter with him while you are on the way, so that he won't drag you before the judge, and the judge hand you over to the police, and the police put you in jail. ⁵⁹You will not come out of there, I tell you, until you pay the last penny of your fine."

Turn from Your Sins or Die

13 At that time some people were there who told Jesus about the Galileans whom Pilate had killed while they were offering sacrifices to God. ²Jesus answered them: "Because these Galileans were killed in that way, do you think it proves that they were worse sinners than all the other Galileans? ³No! I tell you that if you do not turn from your sins, you will all die as they did. ⁴What about those eighteen in Siloam who were killed when the tower fell on them? Do you suppose this proves that they were worse than all the other people living in Jerusalem? ⁵No! I tell you that if you do not turn from your sins, you will all die as they did."

⁶Then Jesus told them this parable: "A man had a fig tree growing in his vineyard. He went looking for figs on it but found none. ⁷So he said to his gardener, 'Look, for three years I have been coming here looking for figs on this fig tree and I haven't found any. Cut it down! Why should it go on using up the soil? ⁸But the gardener answered, 'Leave it alone, sir, just this one year; I will dig a trench around it and fill it up with fertilizer. ⁹Then if the tree bears figs next year, so much the better; if not, then you will have it cut down.' "

Jesus Heals a Crippled Woman on the Sabbath

¹⁰One Sabbath day Jesus was teaching in a synagogue. ¹¹A woman was there who had an evil spirit in her that had kept her sick for eighteen years; she was bent over and could not straighten up at all. ¹²When Jesus saw her he called out to her, "Woman, you are free from your sickness!" ¹³He placed his hands on her and at once she straightened herself up and praised God. ¹⁴The official of the synagogue was angry that Jesus had healed on the Sabbath; so he spoke up and said to the people, "There are six days in which we should work; so come during those days and be healed, but not on the Sabbath!" ¹⁵The Lord answered him by saying: "You impostors! Any one of you would untie his ox or his donkey from the stall and take it out to give it water on the Sabbath. ¹⁶Now here is this descendant of Abraham whom Satan has kept in bonds for eighteen years; should she not be freed from her bonds on the Sabbath?" ¹⁷His answer made all his enemies ashamed of themselves, while all the people rejoiced over every wonderful thing that he did.

[18]Jesus said: "What is the Kingdom of God like? What can I compare it with? [19]It is like a mustard seed, which a man took and planted in his field; the plant grew and became a tree, and the birds made their nests in its branches."

[20]Again Jesus asked: "What shall I compare the Kingdom of God with? [21]It is like the yeast which a woman takes and mixes in a bushel of flour, until the whole batch of dough rises."

The Narrow Door
(Also Matt. 7.13–14, 21–23)

[22]Jesus went through towns and villages, teaching and making his way toward Jerusalem. [23]Someone asked him, "Sir, will just a few people be saved?" Jesus answered them: [24]"Do your best to go in through the narrow door; for many people, I tell you, will try to go in but will not be able.

[25]"The master of the house will get up and close the door; then when you stand outside and begin to knock on the door and say, 'Open the door for us, sir!' he will answer you, 'I don't know where you come from!' [26]Then you will answer back, 'We ate and drank with you; you taught in our town!' [27]He will say again, 'I don't know where you come from. Get away from me, all you evil-doers!' [28]What crying and gnashing of teeth there will be when you see Abraham, Isaac, and Jacob and all the prophets in the Kingdom of God, while you are kept outside! [29]People will come from the east and the west, from the north and the south, and sit at the table in the Kingdom of God. [30]Then those who are now last will be first, and who are now first will be last."

■ Discussion

1. Based on your understanding of 10:1–24, what are the theological foundations of the Church's mission?
2. What life-style should characterize those who devote themselves to the Church's mission?
3. Reread 10:25–11:13. What does it mean to love one's neighbor? What does it mean to love God? How are love of God and love of neighbor related?
4. How should we approach God in prayer?
5. In this section of the Gospel, what value does Jesus place on material wealth and personal satisfaction?

■ Prayer and Meditation

"I the LORD have called you and given you power
　　to see that justice is done on earth.
Through you I will make a covenant with all peoples;
　　through you I will bring light to the nations.
You will open the eyes of the blind
　　and set free those who sit in dark prisons."

Isaiah 42:6–7

The Journey Proceeds/ and Ends —— Luke 13:31—21:38

As the journey proceeds, Jesus departs from Galilee, not because he feared Herod Antipas, but rather because the goal of his travel was a prophet's death in Jerusalem (13:31–35). Luke quite deliberately organized his account so that earlier key events in Galilee would foreshadow the most important part of the Gospel—Jesus' passion, death, and resurrection. Like the Old Testament prophets before him, Jesus would be rejected by his own people and killed in Jerusalem.

Banquet Teachings

The banquet in the house of a powerful Pharisee is the occasion for Jesus' teachings about the kingdom of God in 14:1–24. In every human culture, sharing a meal produces a special bond between people. In the ancient Near East, the meal was a very important sign of hospitality and respect. In the Old Testament, the making of covenants or agreements, offering sacrifices, and sharing wisdom took place in the context of meals.

In the time of Jesus, the future kingdom of God was frequently pictured as a banquet at which the Messiah presided. One of the most striking and controversial features of Jesus' public life was his practice of sharing meals with tax collectors and sinners. These meals symbolized the reconciliation with God that Jesus came to offer even the outsiders of society.

The healing of the man afflicted with dropsy (14:1–6) takes place at the banquet in a Pharisee's house. The strict observance of the rules of work on the Sabbath was very important to the Pharisees, and banquets were occasions at which they celebrated their religious fellowship. Thus Jesus' healing activity on the Sabbath at a pharisaic banquet was doubly shocking.

The banquet provides the occasion for Jesus to share his wisdom with the other guests in 14:7–14. The first instruction (14:7–11) involves choosing places of honor at a banquet. The kingdom of God was often pictured as a banquet, and this image led to speculations about who would occupy the most prestigious places in the kingdom.

Jesus' Love for Jerusalem
(Also Matt. 23.37–39)

[31]At that same time some Pharisees came to Jesus and said to him, "You must get out of here and go somewhere else, for Herod wants to kill you." [32]Jesus answered them: "Go tell that fox: 'I am driving out demons and performing cures today and tomorrow, and on the third day I shall finish my work.' [33]Yet I must be on my way today, tomorrow and the next day; it is not right for a prophet to be killed anywhere except in Jerusalem.

[34]"O Jerusalem, Jerusalem! You kill the prophets, you stone the messengers God has sent you! How many times I wanted to put my arms around all your people, just as a hen

gathers her chicks under her wings, but you would not let me! [35]Now your home will be completely forsaken. You will not see me, I tell you, until the time comes when you say, 'God bless him who comes in the name of the Lord.' "

Jesus Heals a Sick Man

14 One Sabbath day Jesus went to eat a meal at the home of one of the leading Pharisees; and people were watching Jesus closely. [2]A man whose legs and arms were swollen came to Jesus, [3]and Jesus spoke up and asked the teachers of the Law and the Pharisees, "Does our Law allow healing on the Sabbath, or not?" [4]But they would not say a thing. Jesus took the man, healed him and sent him away. [5]Then he said to them, "If any one of you had a son or an ox that happened to fall in a well on a Sabbath, would you not pull him out at once on the Sabbath itself?" [6]But they were not able to answer him about this.

Humility and Hospitality

[7]Jesus noticed how some of the guests were choosing the best places, so he told this parable to all of them: [8]"When someone invites you to a wedding feast, do not sit down in the best place. For it could happen that someone more important than you had been invited, [9]and your host, who invited both of you, would come and say to you, 'Let him have this place.' Then you would be ashamed and have to sit in the lowest place. [10]Instead, when you are invited, go and sit in the lowest place, so that your host will come to you and say, 'Come on

up, my friend, to a better place.' This will bring you honor in the presence of all the other guests. ¹¹For everyone who makes himself great will be humbled, and whoever humbles himself will be made great."

¹²Then Jesus said to his host: "When you give a lunch or a dinner, do not invite your friends, or your brothers, or your relatives, or your rich neighbors—for they will invite you back and in this way you will be paid for what you did. ¹³When you give a feast, invite the poor, the crippled, the lame, and the blind, ¹⁴and you will be blessed; for they are not able to pay you back. You will be paid by God when the good people are raised from death."

The second instruction concerns the kind of people to be invited to the banquet. Belief in the resurrection of the dead and in rewards and punishments at the last judgment was very strong among the Pharisees. So Jesus challenges his host to act on his belief.

If there were any doubt at all that these banquet instructions were to be understood as relating to the kingdom of God, it is swept away by the parable of the great supper in 14:15–24. The parable reflects God's invitation to his people Israel through the prophets. Time and again in the Old Testament the prophets proclaimed God's message to the Israelites, and the message was repeatedly ignored. Now the invitation is offered to the poor and the outcasts of society, certainly a reflection and a justification of Jesus' life-style. Those who reject the invitation of the Gospel shall not partake in the kingdom.

After the banquet, Jesus makes clear the challenges involved in following him (14:25–35). In 14:26, he cites the extreme example of disruption in family relationships, as he did in 9:59–62. Then Jesus uses the image of the cross to describe the degree of dedication required of his disciples. There is in this passage both a prediction of the manner of Jesus' death, and a verification for the Christians of Luke's time of the demands of discipleship. Those who think that they want to follow Jesus are urged to count the costs beforehand. This is made clear by the parables of the tower-builder and the king going out to war (14:28–32).

The teaching on the challenge of discipleship ends with sayings on renunciation (14:33) and salt (14:34–35). The saying on salt is very obscure, but it probably refers to the wisdom of Christians and their role as the salt of the earth.

■ *Reflection*
What are the costs of discipleship in the contemporary Church?

The Parable of the Great Feast
(Also Matt. 22.1–10)

15One of the men sitting at the table heard this and said to Jesus, "How happy are those who will sit at the table in the Kingdom of God!" 16Jesus said to him: "There was a man who was giving a great feast, to which he invited many people. 17At the time for the feast he sent his servant to tell his guests, 'Come, everything is ready!' 18But they all began, one after another, to make excuses. The first one told the servant, 'I bought a field, and have to go and look at it; please accept my apologies.' 19Another one said, 'I bought five pairs of oxen and am on my way to try them out; please accept my apologies.' 20Another one said, 'I have just gotten married, and for this reason I cannot come.' 21The servant went back and told all this to his master. The master of the house was furious and said to his servant, 'Hurry out to the streets and alleys of the town, and bring back the poor, the crippled, the blind, and the lame.' ²²Soon the servant said, 'Your order has been carried out, sir, but there is room for more.' ²³So the master said to the servant, 'Go out to the country roads and lanes, and make people come in, so that my house will be full. ²⁴None of those men who were invited, I tell you all, will taste my dinner!' "

The Cost of Being a Disciple
(Also Matt. 10.37–38)

²⁵Great crowds of people were going along with Jesus. He turned and said to them: ²⁶"Whoever comes to me cannot be my disciple unless he hates his father and his mother, his wife and his children, his brothers and his sisters, and himself as well. ²⁷Whoever does not carry his own cross and come after me cannot be my disciple. ²⁸If one of you is planning to build a tower, he sits down first and figures out what it will cost, to see if he has enough money to finish the job. ²⁹If he doesn't, he will not be able to finish the tower after laying the foundation; and all who see what happened will make fun of him. ³⁰'This man began to build but can't finish the job!' they will say. ³¹If a king goes out with ten thousand men to fight another king, who comes against him with twenty thousand men, he will sit down first and decide if he is strong enough to face that other king. ³²If he isn't, he will have to send messengers to meet the other king, while he is still a long way off, to ask for terms of peace. ³³In the same way," concluded Jesus, "none of you can be my disciple unless he gives up everything he has."

³⁴"Salt is good, but if it loses its taste there is no way to make it good again. ³⁵It is no good for the soil or for the manure pile; it is thrown away. Listen, then, if you have ears!''

Parables of the Lost

The parables of the lost sheep, the lost coin, and the lost son (15:4–32) explain Jesus' practice of seeking out sinners and reconciling them with God. The scene is set in 15:1–3. The tax collectors were suspected of personal dishonesty and treason for collaborating with the Romans, and the sinners made up a social class that paid no attention to the detailed demands of the Old Testament law. The Pharisees were religious purists who took very seriously the observance of the law and looked down on those who did not. The scribes were the experts in interpreting the law. The three parables explain to the Pharisees and the scribes why Jesus paid attention to the tax collectors and the sinners.

The parable of the lost sheep expresses God's joy over a repentant sinner. It is a direct answer to the Pharisees' objection to Jesus' habit of taking meals with those who were considered to be sinners and outcasts by those who prided themselves on keeping the Jewish law. The parable implies that Jesus is doing God's will in welcoming sinners back to the fold.

The parable of the lost coin (15:8–10) has the same structure and makes the same point as the preceding parable. In 15:10 Jesus relates the two parables with a similar closing statement.

The parable of the lost son is better described as the parable of the loving father, since the main character is the father and the focus of the story is the father's love and joy over the prodigal son's return. The first part (15:12–24) concerns the father and the younger son.

The second part (15:25–32) concerns the father and the older son. The older son represents people like the scribes and the Pharisees who were offended by Jesus' offer of reconciliation with God to tax collectors and sinners. Like the older son, the scribes and Pharisees should rejoice over Jesus' ministry, because he is doing God's will, exactly what they are asking people to do.

■ *Reflection*

What attitude should we have toward the sacrament of Reconciliation? Is it necessary for forgiveness?

The Lost Sheep
(Also Matt. 18.12–14)

15 One time many tax collectors and out-casts came to listen to Jesus. ²The Pharisees and the teachers of the Law started grumbling, "This man welcomes outcasts and even eats with them!" ³So Jesus told them this parable: ⁴"Suppose one of you has a hundred sheep and loses one of them—what does he do? He leaves the ninety-nine sheep in the pasture and goes looking for the lost sheep until he finds it. ⁵When he finds it, he is so happy that he puts it on his shoulders, ⁶carries it back home, and calls his friends and neighbors to-gether. 'Rejoice with me,' he tells them, 'for I have found my lost sheep!' In the same way, I tell you, there will be more joy in heaven over one sinner who repents than over ninety-nine respectable people who do not need to repent."

The Lost Coin

[8]"Or suppose a woman who has ten silver coins loses one of them—what does she do? She lights a lamp, sweeps her house, and looks carefully everywhere until she finds it. [9]When she finds it, she calls her friends and neighbors together. 'Rejoice with me,' she tells them, 'for I have found the coin I lost!' [10]In the same way, I tell you, the angels of God rejoice over one sinner who repents."

The Lost Son

[11]Jesus went on to say: "There was a man who had two sons. [12]The younger one said to his father, 'Father, give me now my share of the property.' So the father divided the property between his two sons. [13]After a few days the younger son sold his part of the property and left home with the money. He went to a country far away where he wasted his money in reckless living. [14]He spent everything he had. Then a severe famine spread over that country, and he was left without a thing. [15]So he went to work for one of the citizens of that country, who sent him out to his farm to take care of the pigs. [16]He wished he could fill himself with the bean pods the pigs ate, but no one gave him any. [17]At last he came to his senses and said: 'All my father's hired workers have more than they can eat, and here I am, about to starve! [18]I will get up and go to my father and say, "Father, I have sinned against God and against you. [19]I am no longer fit to be called your son; treat me as one of your hired workers." ' [20]So he got up and started back to his father.

"He was still a long way from home when his father saw him; his heart was filled with pity and he ran, threw his arms around his son, and kissed him. ²¹'Father,' the son said, 'I have sinned against God and against you. I am no longer fit to be called your son.' ²²But the father called his servants: 'Hurry!' he said. 'Bring the best robe and put it on him. Put a ring on his finger and shoes on his feet. ²³Then go get the prize calf and kill it, and let us celebrate with a feast! ²⁴For this son of mine was dead, but now he is alive; he was lost, but now he has been found.' And so the feasting began.

²⁵"The older son, in the meantime, was out in the field. On his way back, when he came close to the house, he heard the music and dancing. ²⁶He called one of the servants and asked him, 'What's going on?' ²⁷'Your brother came back home,' the servant answered, 'and your father killed the prize calf, because he got him back safe and sound.' ²⁸The older brother was so angry that he would not go into the house; so his father came out and begged him to come in. ²⁹'Look,' he answered back to his father, 'all these years I have worked like a slave for you, and not once did I disobey an order of yours. What have you given me? Not even a goat for me to have a feast with my friends! ³⁰But this son of yours wasted all your property on prostitutes, and when he comes back home you kill the prize calf for him!' ³¹'My son,' the father answered, 'you are always at home and everything I have is yours. ³²But we had to have a feast and be happy, for your brother was dead, but now he is alive; he was lost, but now he has been found.' "

Teachings About Wealth

Much of the material in Luke 16 deals with money. The first part (16:1–13) consists of the parable of the dishonest manager (16:1–8) and three sayings on attitudes toward wealth (16:9–13). The parable may have been based on an actual incident brought to Jesus' attention. It was expected that his reaction would be negative, but he surprised his audience by using the manager's clever action as a challenge to show cleverness in spiritual matters.

The manager represented the interests of an absentee landlord or someone with a large business operation. He may have been receiving a commission or a percentage back from collecting his master's debts. Thus he would have the right to reduce the amount of the debt by foregoing his part of the return. The behavior emphasized in the parable is cleverness, not dishonesty.

In 16:9–13 we have three sayings concerning the proper attitudes toward money. The proper use of earthly goods is presented as the condition for receiving heavenly goods. If you cannot deal properly with money, you cannot expect to receive heavenly goods. In 16:13 we are warned not to let money become so important that it takes the place of God.

In the context of an attack on the Pharisees (16:14–15), Jesus puts forth teachings on God's plan of redemption, the Old Testament, and divorce (16:16–18). The saying about the plan of redemption distinguishes the time of Jesus (when the good news of the kingdom is preached) from the time of the Old Testament. Luke asserts that John the Baptist belonged to the period of the Old Testament.

The saying on divorce and remarriage (16:18) emphasizes the indissolubility of marriage. This was as revolutionary a teaching in Jesus' time as it is today. Divorce was an accepted institution in New Testament times, and there is evidence (Matthew 5:32; 19:9, and 1 Corinthians 7:12–16) that the early Church took a slightly more lenient view than Luke and Mark have expressed in their Gospels.

The story of Lazarus and the rich man (16:19–31) carries on the theme of the exaltation of the lowly and the humbling of the rich. It also provides a chilling warning to those who believe that material wealth is God's stamp of approval. The two main characters are contrasted. Lazarus illustrates Jesus blessing in 6:20: "Happy are you poor; the kingdom of God is yours!" The rich man illustrates Jesus' warning in 6:24: "But how terrible for you who are rich now; you have had your easy life!"

The second part of the story (16:24–31) is a dialogue between the rich man and Abraham. The dialogue has more than one level of meaning. On the one hand, the Jewish leaders are reminded of the preaching of Moses and the prophets, of the law which they do not observe in spirit; on the other hand, the Jews of Luke's time are chastised because they do not believe even though Christ has been raised from the dead. Jesus preached the same concern for the poor as did the prophets of old.

The Shrewd Manager

16 Jesus said to his disciples: "There was a rich man who had a manager, and he was told that the manager was wasting his master's money. ²He called him in and said, 'What is this I hear about you? Turn in a complete account of your handling of my property, for you cannot be my manager any longer.' ³'My master is about to dismiss me from my job,' the man said to himself. 'What shall I do? I am not strong enough to dig ditches, and I am ashamed to beg. ⁴Now I know what I will do! Then when my job is gone I shall have friends who will welcome me in their homes.' ⁵So he called in all the people who were in debt to his master. To the first one he said, 'How much do you owe my master?' ⁶'One hundred barrels of olive oil,' he answered. 'Here is your account,' the manager told him; 'sit down and write fifty.' ⁷To another one he said, 'And you—how much do you owe?' 'A thousand bushels of wheat,' he answered. 'Here is your account,' the manager told him; 'write eight hundred.' ⁸The master of this dishonest manager praised him for doing such a shrewd thing; for the people of this world are much more shrewd in handling their affairs than the people who belong to the light.''

⁹And Jesus went on to say: ''And so I tell you: make friends for yourselves with worldly wealth, so that when it gives out you will be welcomed in the eternal home. ¹⁰Whoever is faithful in small matters will be faithful in large ones; whoever is dishonest in small matters will be dishonest in large ones. ¹¹If, then, you have not been faithful in handling worldly wealth, how can you be trusted with true wealth? ¹²And if you have not been faithful in what belongs to someone else, who will give you what belongs to you?

¹³''No servant can be the slave of two masters: he will hate one and love the other; he will be loyal to one and despise the other. You cannot serve both God and money.''

Some Sayings of Jesus
(Also Matt. 11.12–13; 5.31–32; Mark 10.11–12)

¹⁴The Pharisees heard all this, and they made fun of Jesus, because they loved money. ¹⁵Jesus said to them: "You are the ones who make yourselves look right in men's sight, but God knows your hearts. For what men think is of great value is worth nothing in God's sight.

¹⁶"The Law of Moses and the writings of the prophets were in effect up to the time of John the Baptist; since then the Good News about the Kingdom of God is being told, and everyone forces his way in. ¹⁷But it is easier for heaven and earth to disappear than for the smallest detail of the Law to be done away with.

¹⁸"Any man who divorces his wife and marries another woman commits adultery; and the man who marries a divorced woman commits adultery."

The Rich Man and Lazarus

¹⁹"There was once a rich man who dressed in the most expensive clothes and lived in great luxury every day. ²⁰There was also a poor man, named Lazarus, full of sores, who used to be brought to the rich man's door, ²¹hoping to fill himself with the bits of food that fell from the rich man's table. Even the dogs would come and lick his sores. ²²The poor man died and was carried by the angels to Abraham's side, at the feast in heaven; the rich man died and was buried. ²³He was in great pain in Hades; and he looked up and saw Abraham, far away, with Lazarus at his side. ²⁴So he called out, 'Father Abraham! Take pity on me, and send Lazarus to dip his finger in some water and cool off my

tongue, for I am in great pain in this fire!' ²⁵But Abraham said: 'Remember, my son, that in your lifetime you were given all the good things, while Lazarus got all the bad things; but now he is enjoying it here, while you are in pain. ²⁶Besides all that, there is a deep pit lying between us, so that those who want to cross over from here to you cannot do it, nor can anyone cross over to us from where you are.' ²⁷The rich man said, 'Well, father, I beg you, send Lazarus to my father's house, ²⁸where I have five brothers; let him go and warn them so that they, at least, will not come to this place of pain.' ²⁹Abraham said, 'Your brothers have Moses and the prophets to warn them; let your brothers listen to what they say.' ³⁰The rich man answered, 'That is not enough, father Abraham! But if someone were to rise from death and go to them, then they would turn from their sins.' ³¹But Abraham said, 'If they will not listen to Moses and the prophets, they will not be convinced even if someone were to rise from death.' ''

The Journey Ends

As the journey up to Jerusalem nears its goal, Jesus warns his disciples against being the occasions of another person's sin (17:1–2), urges them to offer forgiveness freely and repeatedly to repentant sinners (17:3–4), emphasizes the enormous power of even a little faith (17:5–6), and tells them to look on themselves as servants who are only doing their duty (17:7–10). The story of the ten lepers (17:11–19) not only illustrates the pleasing quality of giving thanks to God but also suggests that an outsider like the Samaritan can do the right thing where Judeans and Galileans fail (see 10:29–37).

Having sketched some of the disicples' responsibilities, Jesus turns to the coming of the kingdom in 17:20–37. He rules out speculations regarding the signs and the times. When the kingdom comes, it will be clear to all and sudden. People should not be fooled by the lack of signs, since no signs preceded the flood in Noah's time or the destruction of Sodom. The coming of the Son of Man will be so fast that there will be no turning back. It will be decisive in its results.

Two additional instructions on prayer are provided in the parables of the unjust judge and the persistent widow (18:1–8) and in the parable of the Pharisee and the tax collector (18:9–14). If an unjust judge finally gives in to the untiring requests of the persistent widow, will not God hear those who pray to him? The contrast between the self-righteous Pharisee and the humble tax collector encourages humility before God in prayer. The two parables emphasize some surprising things about prayer: shameless persistence pays off (see 11:5–13), and the prayers of "unlikely" persons are heard.

■ *Reflection*
Do we believe that our prayers are always answered? Do we always pray for the right things?

Sin
(Also Matt. 18.6–7, 21–22; Mark 9.42)

17 Jesus said to his disciples: "Things that make people fall into sin are bound to happen; but how terrible for the one who makes them happen! ²It would be better for him if a large millstone were tied around his neck and he were thrown into the sea, than for him to cause one of these little ones to sin. ³Be on your guard!

"If your brother sins, rebuke him, and if he repents, forgive him. ⁴If he sins against you seven times in one day, and each time he comes to you saying, 'I repent,' you must forgive him."

⁵The apostles said to the Lord, "Make our faith greater." ⁶The Lord answered: "If you had faith as big as a mustard seed, you could say to this mulberry tree, 'Pull yourself up by the roots and plant yourself in the sea!' and it would obey you."

A Servant's Duty

⁷"Suppose one of you has a servant who is plowing or looking after the sheep. When he comes in from the field, do you say to him, 'Hurry along and eat your meal'? ⁸Of course not! Instead, you say to him, 'Get my supper ready, then put on your apron and wait on me while I eat and drink; after that you may eat and drink.' ⁹The servant does not deserve thanks for obeying orders, does he? ¹⁰It is the same with you; when you have done all you have been told to do, say, 'We are ordinary servants; we have only done our duty.' "

Jesus Heals Ten Men

¹¹As Jesus made his way to Jerusalem he went between Samaria and Galilee. ¹²He was going into a certain village when he was met by ten lepers. They stood at a distance ¹³and shouted, "Jesus! Master! Have pity on us!" ¹⁴Jesus saw them and said to them, "Go and let the priests examine you." On the way they were made clean. ¹⁵One of them, when he saw

that he was healed, came back, praising God with a loud voice. [16]He threw himself to the ground at Jesus' feet, thanking him. The man was a Samaritan. [17]Jesus spoke up: "There were ten men made clean; where are the other nine? [18]Why is this foreigner the only one who came back to give thanks to God?" [19]And Jesus said to him, "Get up and go; your faith has made you well."

The Coming of the Kingdom
(Also Matt. 24.23–28, 37–41)

[20]Some Pharisees asked Jesus when the Kingdom of God would come. His answer was: "The Kingdom of God does not come in such a way as to be seen. [21]No one will say, 'Look, here it is!' or, 'There it is!'; because the Kingdom of God is within you."

[22]Then he said to the disciples: "The time will come when you will wish you could see one of the days of the Son of Man, but you will not see it. [23]There will be those who will say to you, 'Look, over there!' or, 'Look, over here!' But don't go out looking for it. [24]As the lightning flashes across the sky and lights it up from one side to the other, so will the Son of Man be in his day. [25]But first he must suffer much and be rejected by the people of this day. [26]As it was in the time of Noah, so shall it be in the days of the Son of Man. [27]Everybody kept on eating and drinking, men and women married, up to the very day Noah went into the ark and the Flood came and killed them all. [28]It will be as it was in the time of Lot. Everybody kept on eating and drinking, buying and selling, planting and building. [29]On the day Lot left Sodom, fire and sulphur rained down from heaven and killed

them all. ³⁰That is how it will be on the day the Son of Man is revealed.

³¹"The man who is on the roof of his house on that day must not go down into his house to get his belongings that are there; in the same way, the man who is out in the field must not go back to the house. ³²Remember Lot's wife! ³³Whoever tries to save his own life will lose it; whoever loses his life will save it. ³⁴On that night, I tell you, there will be two men sleeping in one bed: one will be taken away, the other left behind. ³⁵Two women will be grinding meal together: one will be taken away, the other left behind. [³⁶Two men will be in the field, one will be taken away, the other left behind.]" ³⁷The disciples asked him, "Where, Lord?" Jesus answered, "Where there is a dead body the vultures will gather."

The Parable of the Widow and the Judge

18 Then Jesus told them this parable, to teach them that they should always pray and never become discouraged. ²"There was a judge in a certain town who neither feared God nor respected men. ³And there was a widow in that same town who kept coming to him and pleading for her rights: 'Help me against my opponent!' ⁴For a long time the judge was not willing, but at last he said to himself, 'Even though I don't fear God or respect men, ⁵yet because of all the trouble this widow is giving me I will see to it that she gets her rights; or else she will keep on coming and finally wear me out!' " ⁶And the Lord continued: "Listen to what that corrupt judge said. ⁷Now, will God not judge in favor of his own

people who cry to him for help day and night? Will he be slow to help them? [8]I tell you, he will judge in their favor, and do it quickly. But will the Son of Man find faith on earth when he comes?''

The Parable of the Pharisee and the Tax Collector

[9]Jesus also told this parable to people who were sure of their own goodness and despised everybody else. [10]''Two men went up to the Temple to pray; one was a Pharisee, the other a tax collector. [11]The Pharisee stood apart by himself and prayed: 'I thank you, God, that I am not greedy, dishonest, or immoral, like everybody else; I thank you that I am not like that tax collector. [12]I fast two days every week, and I give you one tenth of all my income.' [13]But the tax collector stood at a distance and would not even raise his face to heaven, but beat on his breast and said, 'O God, have pity on me, a sinner!' [14]I tell you,'' said Jesus, ''this man, and not the other, was in the right with God when he went home. For everyone who makes himself great will be humbled, and everyone who humbles himself will be made great.''

From this point on, Luke rejoins the outline set by Mark 10:13—16:8. The kingdom of God must be received as a gift (18:15—17), just as children who depend totally on their parents necessarily receive everything as a gift. Entering the kingdom of God may involve giving away all earthly goods (18:18—23). Wealth seems to be a great obstacle to discipleship (18:24—27), but sacrificing wealth will be richly rewarded now and in the future (18:28—30). As they near Jerusalem, Jesus again predicts his death and resurrection in 18:31–34 (see 9:22; 9:44), and again the disciples fail to understand. Near Jericho a blind beggar is given sight and joins Jesus on his way to Jerusalem.

The encounter with Zacchaeus the tax collector in 19:1–10 illustrates once more that suspect social status and occupation do not prevent one from being a follower of Jesus. Even though many people considered Zacchaeus a sinner, he was (or resolved to become) a charitable and honest man. In Jesus the saving power of God is present and offered to all kinds of people. The parable of the talents (19:11–27) demands that bold and fruitful action be taken in the face of the coming kingdom. Watchfulness must not be mistaken for cowardice or laziness. The goal of the journey is finally reached in the account of Jesus' entry into Jerusalem (19:28–38) and his sad prediction of its destruction (19:39–44).

Jesus Blesses Little Children
(Also Matt. 19.13–15; Mark 10.13–16)

[15]Some people brought their babies to Jesus to have him place his hands on them. But the disciples saw them and scolded them for doing so. [16]But Jesus called the children to him, and said: "Let the children come to me! Do not stop them, because the Kingdom of God belongs to such as these. [17]Remember this! Whoever does not receive the Kingdom of God like a child will never enter it."

[18]A certain Jewish leader asked him: "Good Teacher, what must I do to receive eternal life?" [19]"Why do you call me good?" Jesus asked him. "No one is good except God alone. [20]You know the commandments: 'Do not commit adultery; do not murder; do not steal; do

not lie; honor your father and mother.' " ²¹The man replied, "Ever since I was young I have obeyed all these commandments." ²²When Jesus heard this, he said to him: "You still need to do one thing. Sell all you have and give the money to the poor, and you will have riches in heaven; then come and follow me." ²³But when the man heard this he became very sad, because he was very rich.

²⁴Jesus saw that he was sad and said; "How hard it is for rich people to enter the Kingdom of God! ²⁵It is much harder for a rich man to enter the Kingdom of God than for a camel to go through the eye of a needle." ²⁶The people who heard him asked, "Who, then, can be saved?" ²⁷Jesus answered, "What is impossible for men is possible for God."

²⁸Then Peter said, "Look! We have left our homes to follow you." ²⁹"Yes," Jesus said to them, "and I tell you this: anyone who leaves home or wife or brothers or parents or children for the sake of the Kingdom of God ³⁰will receive much more in the present age, and eternal life in the age to come."

³¹Jesus took the twelve disciples aside and said to them: "Listen! We are going to Jerusalem where everything the prophets wrote about the Son of Man will come true. ³²He will be handed over to the Gentiles, who will make fun of him, insult him, and spit on him. ³³They will whip him and kill him, but on the third day he will be raised to life." ³⁴The disciples did not understand any of these things; the meaning of the words was hidden from them, and they did not know what Jesus was talking about.

Jesus Heals a Blind Beggar
(Also Matt. 20.29–34; Mark 10.46–52)

³⁵Jesus was coming near Jericho, and a certain blind man was sitting and begging by the road. ³⁶When he heard the crowd passing by he asked, "What is this?" ³⁷"Jesus of Nazareth is passing by," they told him. ³⁸He cried out, "Jesus! Son of David! Have mercy on me!" ³⁹The people in front scolded him and told him to be quiet. But he shouted even more loudly, "Son of David! Have mercy on me!" ⁴⁰So Jesus stopped and ordered that the blind man be brought to him. When he came near, Jesus asked him, ⁴¹"What do you want me to do for you?" "Sir," he answered, "I want to see again." ⁴²Then Jesus said to him, "See! Your faith has made you well." ⁴³At once he was able to see, and he followed Jesus, giving thanks to God. When the crowd saw it, they all praised God.

Jesus and Zacchaeus

19 Jesus went on into Jericho and was passing through. ²There was a chief tax collector there, named Zacchaeus, who was rich. ³He was trying to see who Jesus was, but he was a little man and could not see Jesus because of the crowd. ⁴So he ran ahead of the crowd and climbed a sycamore tree to see Jesus, who would be going that way. ⁵When Jesus came to that place he looked up and said to Zacchaeus, "Hurry down, Zacchaeus, for I must stay in your house today." ⁶Zacchaeus hurried down and welcomed him with great joy. ⁷All the people who saw it started grumbling, "This man has gone as a guest to the home of a sinner!" ⁸Zacchaeus stood up and

said to the Lord, "Listen, sir! I will give half my belongings to the poor; and if I have cheated anyone, I will pay him back four times as much." ⁹Jesus said to him, "Salvation has come to this house today; this man, also, is a descendant of Abraham. ¹⁰For the Son of Man came to seek and to save the lost."

The Parable of the Gold Coins
(Also Matt. 25.14–30)

¹¹Then Jesus told a parable to those who heard him say this. He was now almost at Jerusalem, and they supposed that the Kingdom of God was just about to appear. ¹²So he said: "There was a nobleman who went to a country far away to be made king and then come back home. ¹³Before he left, he called his ten servants and gave them each a gold coin and told them, 'See what you can earn with this while I am gone.' ¹⁴Now, his countrymen hated him, and so they sent messengers after him to say, 'We don't want this man to be our king.'

¹⁵"The nobleman was made king and came back. At once he ordered his servants, to whom he had given the money, to appear before him in order to find out how much they had earned. ¹⁶The first one came up and said, 'Sir, I have earned ten gold coins with the one you gave me.' ¹⁷'Well done,' he said; 'you are a good servant! Since you were faithful in small matters, I will put you in charge of ten cities.' ¹⁸The second servant came and said, 'Sir, I have earned five gold coins with the one you gave me.' ¹⁹To this one he said, 'You will be in charge of five cities.' ²⁰Another servant came and said: 'Sir, here is your gold coin; I kept it hidden in a handkerchief. ²¹I was afraid of you, because you

are a hard man. You take what is not yours, and reap what you did not plant.' ²²He said to him: 'You bad servant! I will use your own words to condemn you! You know that I am a hard man, taking what is not mine and reaping what I have not planted. ²³Well, then, why didn't you put my money in the bank? Then I would have received it back with interest when I returned.' ²⁴Then he said to those who were standing there, 'Take the gold coin away from him and give it to the servant who has ten coins.' ²⁵They said to him, 'Sir, he already has ten coins!' ²⁶'I tell you,' he replied, 'that to every one who has, even more will be given; but the one who does not have, even the little that he has will be taken away from him. ²⁷Now, as for these enemies of mine who did not want me to be their king: bring them here and kill them before me!' ''

The Triumphant Approach to Jerusalem
(Also Matt. 21.1–11; Mark 11.1–11; John 12.12–19)

²⁸Jesus said this and then went on to Jerusalem ahead of them. ²⁹As he came near Bethphage and Bethany, at the Mount of Olives, he sent two disciples ahead ³⁰with these instructions: "Go to the village there ahead of you; as you go in you will find a colt tied up that has never been ridden. Untie it and bring it here. ³¹If someone asks you, 'Why are you untying it?' tell him, 'The Master needs it.' ''
³²They went on their way and found everything just as Jesus had told them. ³³As they were untying the colt, its owners said to them, "Why are you untying it?" ³⁴"The Master needs it," they answered, ³⁵and took the colt to Jesus. Then they threw their cloaks over the animal

and helped Jesus get on. [36]As he rode on, they spread their cloaks on the road. [37]When he came near Jerusalem, at the place where the road went down the Mount of Olives, the large crowd of his disciples began to thank God and praise him in loud voices for all the great things that they had seen: [38]"God bless the king who comes in the name of the Lord! Peace in heaven, and glory to God!"

[39]Then some of the Pharisees spoke up from the crowd to Jesus. "Teacher," they said, "command your disciples to be quiet!" [40]Jesus answered, "If they keep quiet, I tell you, the stones themselves will shout."

[41]He came closer to the city and when he saw it he wept over it, [42]saying: "If you only knew today what is needed for peace! But now you cannot see it! [43]For the days will come upon you when your enemies will surround you with barricades, blockade you, and close in on you from every side. [44]They will completely destroy you and the people within your walls; not a single stone will they leave in its place, because you did not recognize the time when God came to save you!"

Activities in Jerusalem

Luke's account of Jesus' ministry in Jerusalem in 19:45—21:38 follows Mark 11:11—13:37 very closely. By ridding the Temple of its commercialism (19:45–48), Jesus declares it to be "his house" and uses it as the place for his public teaching (see 19:47; 20:1; 21:5–7; 37–38). Another series of controversy stories in 20:1–44 shows what a brilliant teacher Jesus was and why his opponents were so angry at him. These controversies concern the source of Jesus' authority (20:1–8), the relation between Jesus' suffering and death and those of the prophets before him (20:9–19), paying taxes to the Roman emperor (20:20–26), the nature of the resurrection of the dead (20:27–40), and the identity of the son of David (20:41–44). Finally, the ostentatious and hypocritical piety of the scribes (20:45–47) is contrasted with the simple devotion of the poor widow in 21:1–4.

Jesus' public ministry at the Jerusalem Temple concludes with his discourse about the end of the world as we know it and the final coming of God's kingdom. The discourse is set in the framework of Jesus' daily teaching at the Temple (21:5–7, 37–38). In 21:8–19, the immediate future is described in terms of false rumors, cosmic signs, and persecutions. In contrast to Mark 13:9, Luke 21:12 insists that the persecutions will come before the cosmic signs. Furthermore, Luke 21:19 lays special emphasis on patient endurance in the face of persecution.

The second stage in the scenario for the end involves the destruction of Jerusalem (21:20–24). The description reflects the actual destruction of the city and its Temple by the Romans in A.D. 70 (see 19:43–44). Only after the times of the gentiles have been fulfilled will the cosmic upheavals preceding the coming of Jesus as the Son of Man (21:25–27) take place. The discourse concludes with advice concerning attitudes toward these events (21:28–36). For the faithful followers of Jesus, these events will bring redemption rather than destruction. The proper stance is watchfulness.

Jesus Goes to the Temple
(Also Matt. 21.12–17; Mark 11.15–19; John 2.13–22)

⁴⁵Jesus went into the Temple and began to drive out the merchants, ⁴⁶saying to them: "It is written in the Scriptures that God said, 'My house will be called a house of prayer.' But you

have turned it into a hideout for thieves!''

⁴⁷Jesus taught in the Temple every day. The chief priests, the teachers of the Law, and the leaders of the people wanted to kill him, ⁴⁸but they could not find how to do it, because all the people kept listening to him, not wanting to miss a single word.

The Question About Jesus' Authority
(Also Matt. 21.23–27; Mark 11.27–33)

20One day, when Jesus was in the Temple teaching the people and preaching the Good News, the chief priests and the teachers of the Law, together with the elders, came ²and said to him, ''Tell us, what right do you have to do these things? Who gave you the right to do them?'' ³Jesus answered them: ''Now let me ask you a question. Tell me, ⁴did John's right to baptize come from God or from man?'' ⁵They started to argue among themselves: ''What shall we say? If we say, 'From God,' he will say, 'Why, then, did you not believe John?' ⁶But if we say, 'From man,' this whole crowd here will stone us, because they are convinced that John was a prophet.'' ⁷So they answered, ''We don't know where it came from.'' ⁸And Jesus said to them, ''Neither will I tell you, then, by what right I do these things.''

⁹Then Jesus told the people this parable: ''A man planted a vineyard, rented it out to tenants, and then left home for a long time. ¹⁰When the time came for harvesting the grapes, he sent a slave to the tenants to receive from them his share of the harvest. But the tenants beat the slave and sent him back without a thing. ¹¹So he sent another slave, but the tenants beat him also, treated him shamefully,

and sent him back without a thing. ¹²Then he sent a third slave; the tenants hurt him, too, and threw him out. ¹³Then the owner of the vineyard said, 'What shall I do? I will send my own dear son; surely they will respect him!' ¹⁴But when the tenants saw him they said to one another, 'This is the owner's son. Let us kill him, and the vineyard will be ours!' ¹⁵So they threw him out of the vineyard and killed him.

"What, then, will the owner of the vineyard do to the tenants?" Jesus asked. ¹⁶"He will come and kill those men, and turn over the vineyard to other tenants." When the people heard this they said, "Surely not!" ¹⁷Jesus looked at them and asked, "What, then, does this scripture mean?

> 'The stone which the builders rejected as worthless
> Turned out to be the most important stone.'

¹⁸Everyone who falls on that stone will be cut to pieces; and if the stone falls on someone, it will crush him to dust."

The Question About Paying Taxes
(Also Matt. 22.15–22; Mark 12.13–17)

¹⁹The teachers of the Law and the chief priests tried to arrest Jesus on the spot, because they knew that he had told this parable against them; but they were afraid of the people. ²⁰So they watched for the right time. They bribed some men to pretend they were sincere, and sent them to trap Jesus with questions, so they could hand him over to the authority and power of the Governor. ²¹These spies said to Jesus: "Teacher, we know that what you say and teach is right. We know that

you pay no attention to what a man seems to be, but teach the truth about God's will for man. ²²Tell us, is it against our Law for us to pay taxes to the Roman Emperor, or not?" ²³But Jesus saw through their trick and said to them, ²⁴"Show me a silver coin. Whose face and name are these on it?" ²⁵"The Emperor's," they answered. So Jesus said, "Well, then, pay to the Emperor what belongs to him, and pay to God what belongs to God." ²⁶They could not catch him in a thing there before the people, so they kept quiet, amazed at his answer.

The Question About Rising from Death
(Also Matt. 22.23–33; Mark 12.18–27)

²⁷Some Sadducees came to Jesus. (They are the ones who say that people will not rise from death.) They asked him: ²⁸"Teacher, Moses wrote this law for us: 'If a man dies and leaves a wife, but no children, that man's brother must marry the widow so they can have children for the dead man.' ²⁹Once there were seven brothers; the oldest got married, and died without having children. ³⁰Then the second one married the woman, ³¹and then the third; the same thing happened to all seven—they died without having children. ³²Last of all, the woman died. ³³Now, on the day when the dead are raised to life, whose wife will she be? All seven of them had married her!"

³⁴Jesus answered them: "The men and women of this age marry, ³⁵but the men and women who are worthy to be raised from death and live in the age to come do not marry. ³⁶They are like angels and cannot die. They are the sons of God, because they have been raised

from death. ³⁷And Moses clearly proves that the dead will be raised to life. In the passage about the burning bush he speaks of the Lord as 'the God of Abraham, the God of Isaac, and the God of Jacob.' ³⁸This means that he is the God of the living, not of the dead—for all are alive to him." ³⁹Some of the teachers of the Law spoke up, "A good answer, Teacher!" ⁴⁰For they did not dare ask Jesus any more questions.

⁴¹Jesus said to them: "How can it be said that the Messiah will be the descendant of David? ⁴²Because David himself says in the book of Psalms:

'The Lord said to my Lord:
Sit here at my right side,
⁴³Until I put your enemies
As a footstool under your feet.'

⁴⁴David, then, called him 'Lord.' How can the Messiah be David's descendant?"

⁴⁵As the whole crowd listened to him, Jesus said to his disciples: ⁴⁶"Watch out for the teachers of the Law, who like to walk around in their long robes, and love to be greeted with respect in the marketplace; who choose the reserved seats in the synagogues and the best places at feasts; ⁴⁷who take advantage of widows and rob them of their homes, then make a show of saying long prayers! Their punishment will be all the worse!"

The Widow's Offering
(Also Mark 12.41–44)

21 Jesus looked around and saw rich men dropping their gifts in the Temple treasury, ²and he also saw a very poor widow dropping in two little copper coins. ³And he said: "I tell you that this poor widow has really put in more than all the others. ⁴For the others offered their gifts from what they had to spare of their riches; but she, poor as she is, gave all she had to live on.''

Jesus Speaks of the Destruction of the Temple
(Also Matt. 24.1–2; Mark 13.1–2)

⁵Some of them were talking about the Temple, how beautiful it looked with its fine stones and the gifts offered to God. Jesus said, ⁶''All this you see—the time will come when not a single stone here will be left in its place; every one will be thrown down.''

⁷''Teacher,'' they asked, ''when will this be? And what is the sign that will show that the time has come for it to happen?''

⁸Jesus said: ''Watch out; don't be fooled. For many men will come in my name saying, 'I am he!' and, 'The time has come!' But don't follow them. ⁹Don't be afraid when you hear of wars and revolutions; such things must happen first, but they do not mean that the end is near.'' ¹⁰He went on to say: ''One country will fight another country, one kingdom will attack another kingdom; ¹¹there will be terrible earthquakes, famines, and plagues everywhere; there will be awful things and great signs from the sky.

¹²''Before all these things take place, however, you will be arrested and persecuted; you will be handed over to trial in synagogues and be put in prison; you will be brought before kings and rulers for my sake. ¹³This will be your chance to tell the Good News. ¹⁴Make up your minds ahead of time not to worry about

how you will defend yourselves; [15]for I will give you such words and wisdom that none of your enemies will be able to resist or deny what you say. [16]You will be handed over by your parents, your brothers, your relatives, and your friends; they will put some of you to death. [17]Everyone will hate you because of me. [18]But not a single hair from your heads will be lost. [19]Hold firm, for this is how you will save yourselves."

Jesus Speaks of the Destruction of Jerusalem
(Also Matt. 24.15–21; Mark 13.14–19)

[20]"When you see Jerusalem surrounded by armies, then you will know that soon she will be destroyed. [21]Then those who are in Judea must run away to the hills; those who are in the city must leave, and those who are out in the country must not go into the city. [22]For these are 'The Days of Punishment,' to make come true all that the Scriptures say. [23]How terrible it will be in those days for women who are pregnant, and for mothers with little babies! Terrible distress will come upon this land, and God's wrath will be against his people. [24]They will be killed by the sword, and taken as prisoners to all countries, and the heathens will trample over Jerusalem until their time is up."

The Coming of the Son of Man
(Also Matt. 24.29–31; Mark 13.24–27)

[25]"There will be signs in the sun, the moon, and the stars. On earth, whole countries will be in despair, afraid of the roar of the sea and the raging tides. [26]Men will faint from fear as they wait for what is coming over the whole earth;

for the powers in space will be driven from their course. ²⁷Then the Son of Man will appear, coming in a cloud with great power and glory. ²⁸When these things begin to happen, stand up and raise your heads, for your salvation is near."

²⁹Then Jesus told them this parable: "Remember the fig tree and all the other trees. ³⁰When you see their leaves beginning to appear you know that summer is near. ³¹In the same way, when you see these things happening, you will know that the Kingdom of God is about to come.

³²"Remember this! All these things will take place before the people now living have all died. ³³Heaven and earth will pass away; my words will never pass away."

The Need to Watch

³⁴"Watch yourselves! Don't let yourselves become occupied with too much feasting and strong drink, and the worries of this life, or that Day may come on you suddenly. ³⁵For it will come like a trap upon all men over the whole earth. ³⁶Be on watch and pray always that you will have the strength to go safely through all these things that will happen, and to stand before the Son of Man."

³⁷Jesus spent those days teaching in the Temple, and when evening came he would go out and spend the night on the Mount of Olives. ³⁸All the people would go to the Temple early in the morning to listen to him.

■ Discussion

1. What implications do Jesus' teachings at the banquet (14:1–24) have for our understanding of the kingdom?

2. What aspects of the banquet story relate to our understanding of the Eucharist?

3. What can we learn from the parables of the lost sheep, the lost coin, and the lost son in chapter 15 about the relationship between God and sinners?

4. In chapter 16, what are Jesus' teachings concerning sharing? What are the consequences of not sharing?

5. How are Jesus' activities in Jerusalem related to the events in the same city at the time of his birth?

■ Prayer and Meditation

"The LORD says,
'Come, everyone who is thirsty—
   here is water!
Come, you that have no money—
   buy grain and eat!
Come! Buy wine and milk—
   it will cost you nothing!
Why spend money on what does not satisfy?
   Why spend your wages and still be hungry?
Listen to me and do what I say,
   and you will enjoy the best food of all.' "

Isaiah 55:1–2

Martyr
and Example ___ Luke 22:1—24:53

The story of Jesus' suffering, death, and resurrection occupies a climactic place in Luke's Gospel. The evangelist's primary source was Mark 14:1—16:8. To this account he added some independent traditions and his own editorial touches. The result is a narrative in which Jesus, the innocent martyr, puts into practice his own principles of faithfulness to God and love for his enemies. His ministry of proclaiming the good news of the kingdom continues even on the cross. After his death and resurrection, he can be encountered in the Old Testament Scriptures and the community's meals.

The Last Supper

The plot to arrest Jesus (22:1—6) takes place before Passover, one of the important pilgrimage feasts in the Jewish calendar. Since so many people would be on pilgrimage in Jerusalem, it was necessary for Jesus' opponents to find a way of arresting him without touching off a riot. With the collaboration of Judas, they could carry out their plot successfully. Satan reappears at this point in the Gospel. In 4:13, Luke told us that Satan left Jesus for a while, implying his return, this time as a prime cause of Jesus' betrayal and death.

In preparing for the Passover meal (22:7–13), Jesus takes the initiative. He tells Peter and John to go and make the preparations. Luke follows Mark in understanding the Last Supper to have been a Passover meal, though John (and most modern historians) place it on the day before the eight-day celebration began. In any case, the meal took place in the atmosphere of Passover, the celebration of ancient Israel's liberation from slavery in Egypt. The account of the Passover preparation indicates that Jesus was in command of events right from the start of the passion story.

The sharing of the wine and the bread at the Last Supper (22:14–20) provides the occasion for Jesus' farewell discourse (22:21–38). In the company of the apostles, Jesus relates the meal to the future banquet in the kingdom of God. The puzzling sequence of the words over the cup (22:17), and the words over the bread (22:19), and the second words over the cup (22:20) is complicated even more by the fact that some manuscripts omit 22:19b–20 (''which is given . . . sealed with my blood''). These technical problems, however, should not distract us from the many dimensions of the Eucharist opened up by this rich passage. It is a memorial of Jesus' death, a sacrifice, a covenant meal, a Passover meal, and an anticipation of the heavenly banquet.

■ *Reflection*
How can I continue to enrich my appreciation of the Eucharist?

The Plot Against Jesus
(Also Matt. 26.1–5; Mark 14.1–2; John 11.45–53)

22 The time was near for the Feast of Unleavened Bread, which is called the

Passover. ²The chief priests and the teachers of the Law were trying to find some way of killing Jesus; for they were afraid of the people.

Judas Agrees to Betray Jesus
(Also Matt. 26.14–16; Mark 14.10–11)

³Then Satan went into Judas, called Iscariot, who was one of the twelve disciples. ⁴So Judas went off and spoke with the chief priests and the officers of the Temple guard about how he could hand Jesus over to them. ⁵They were pleased and offered to pay him money. ⁶Judas agreed to it and started looking for a good chance to betray Jesus to them without the people knowing about it.

Jesus Prepares to Eat the Passover Meal
(Also Matt. 26.17–25; Mark 14.12–21; John 13.21–30)

⁷The day came during the Feast of Unleavened Bread when the lambs for the Passover meal had to be killed. ⁸Jesus sent Peter and John with these instructions: "Go and get our Passover supper ready for us to eat." ⁹"Where do you want us to get it ready?" they asked him. ¹⁰He said: "Listen! As you go into the city a man carrying a jar of water will meet you. Follow him into the house that he enters, ¹¹and say to the owner of the house: 'The Teacher says to you, Where is the room where my disciples and I will eat the Passover supper?' ¹²He will show you a large furnished room upstairs, where you will get everything ready." ¹³They went off and found everything just as Jesus had told them, and prepared the Passover supper.

The Lord's Supper
(Also Matt. 26.26–30; Mark 14.22–26; I Cor. 11.23–25)

[14]When the hour came, Jesus took his place at the table with the apostles. [15]And he said to them: "I have wanted so much to eat this Passover meal with you before I suffer! [16]For I tell you, I will never eat it until it is given its real meaning in the Kingdom of God." [17]Jesus took the cup, gave thanks to God, and said, "Take this and share it among yourselves; [18]for I tell you that I will not drink this wine from now on until the Kingdom of God comes." [19]Then he took the bread, gave thanks to God, broke it, and gave it to them, saying, "This is my body [which is given for you. Do this in memory of me." [20]In the same way he gave them the cup, after the supper, saying, "This cup is God's new covenant sealed with my blood which is poured out for you.]

Jesus' farewell discourse (22:21–38) shows that Jesus knew beforehand about his betrayal and arrest, that leadership consists in service and humility according to the example of Jesus, and that Jesus was not a political revolutionary. Jesus' remarks look forward to the kingdom of God, not a political kingdom. Whereas he promises positions of prominence in the kingdom to the apostles, he points out that the highest position belongs to the one who serves. Jesus knew beforehand that Peter would betray him. But Jesus prayed, and later Peter became an example of repentance and able to serve and lead the Christian community.

The key to the puzzling conclusion to the farewell discourse in 22:35–38 is the fulfillment of the description of Jesus as the suffering servant of God in Isaiah 53:12: "He was reckoned with transgressors." Just as Jesus was misunderstood as being a criminal, so the disciples' simple and nonviolent missions of 9:1–6 and 10:1–24 had been misunderstood. The instructions by Jesus in 22:36–38 are best understood as "gallows humor," the kind of ironic humor that sometimes comes up in very bleak situations. The point is this: since Jesus and his disciples are reckoned with transgressors (that is, taken for criminals), they may as well act the part.

²¹"But, look! The one who betrays me is here at the table with me! ²²For the Son of Man will die as God has decided it; but how terrible for that man who betrays him!" ²³Then they began to ask among themselves which one of them it could be who was going to do this.

The Argument About Greatness

²⁴An argument came up among the disciples as to which one of them should be thought of as the greatest. ²⁵Jesus said to them: "The kings of this world have power over their people, and the rulers are called 'Friends of the People.' ²⁶But this is not the way it is with you; rather, the greatest one among you must be like the youngest, and the leader must be like the servant. ²⁷Who is greater, the one who sits down to eat or the one who serves him? The one who sits down, of course. But I am among you as one who serves.

²⁸"You have stayed with me all through my trials; ²⁹and just as my Father has given me the right to rule, so I will make the same agreement with you. ³⁰You will eat and drink at my table in my Kingdom, and you will sit on thrones to judge the twelve tribes of Israel."

Jesus Predicts Peter's Denial
(Also Matt. 26.31–35; Mark 14.27–31; John 13.36–38)

³¹"Simon, Simon! Listen! Satan has received permission to test all of you, as a farmer separates the wheat from the chaff. ³²But I have prayed for you, Simon, that your faith will not fail. And when you turn your back to me, you must strengthen your brothers." ³³Peter answered, "Lord, I am ready to go to prison with you and to die with you!" ³⁴"I tell you, Peter," Jesus answered, "the rooster will not crow today until you have said three times that you do not know me."

³⁵Then Jesus said to them, "When I sent you out that time without purse, bag, or shoes, did you lack anything?" "Not a thing," they answered. ³⁶"But now," Jesus said, "whoever has a purse or a bag must take it; and whoever does not have a sword must sell his coat and buy one. ³⁷For I tell you this: the scripture that says 'He was included with the criminals,' must come true about me. For that which was written about me is coming true." ³⁸The disciples said, "Look! Here are two swords, Lord!" "That is enough!" he answered.

Jesus' Prayer and Arrest

The story of Jesus' agony in the garden (22:39–46) presents him as the ideal martyr whose example provides encouragement and guidance for Christians in persecution. The combined warning to the disciples and prayer in 22:40–41, 45–46 has special application to Christians who were undergoing persecution. At the moment of greatest trial, the evangelist tells us that Jesus prayed. For Luke this is a key moment, when Jesus identifies himself as the obedient martyr. The word "agony" in 22:44 refers to the tension and struggle that athletes experience in a contest. The text says that Jesus' sweat came down like drops of blood, not necessarily that he sweated blood.

The arrest of Jesus (22:47–53) shows Jesus as ever faithful to his teaching of nonviolence and to his task as a healer. Jesus reacts to the forces of "the power of darkness" with quiet reproval. He points out the irony of Judas' action, and the underhanded nature of the nighttime arrest. He resists the attempts of his followers to meet violence with violence, and heals the high priest's slave.

Peter's denial of Jesus (22:54–62) and the mockery of Jesus (22:63–65) take place at the house of the high priest. Luke contrasts the insults of the guards with the realization of Jesus' prophecy to Peter. Jesus remains silent because the events speak for themselves.

The Trials

The trial of Jesus before the Jewish council (22:66–71) takes place in the council chambers in the morning. Mark 14:53–72 places the time of the trial at night. In either case, the council is satisfied that its perception of Jesus is correct. He claims to be the Messiah, the heir to David's throne. Their political understanding of this claim leads them to believe that Jesus is a dangerous person, threatening to undo their relationship with the Roman government.

Jesus Prays on the Mount of Olives
(Also Matt. 26.36–46; Mark 14.32–42)

³⁹Jesus left and went, as he usually did, to the Mount of Olives; and the disciples went with him. ⁴⁰When he came to the place he said

to them, "Pray that you will not fall into temptation." [41]Then he went off from them, about the distance of a stone's throw, and knelt down and prayed. [42]"Father," he said, "if you will, take this cup away from me. Not my will, however, but your will be done." [[43]An angel from heaven appeared to him and strengthened him. [44]In great anguish he prayed even more fervently; his sweat was like drops of blood, falling to the ground.]

[45]Rising from his prayer, he went back to the disciples and found them asleep, so great was their grief. [46]And he said to them, "Why are you sleeping? Rise and pray that you will not fall into temptation."

[47]He was still speaking when a crowd arrived; Judas, one of the twelve disciples, was leading them, and he came up to Jesus to kiss him. [48]But Jesus said, "Is it with a kiss, Judas, that you betray the Son of Man?" [49]When the disciples who were with Jesus saw what was going to happen, they said, "Shall we strike with our swords, Lord?" [50]And one of them struck the High Priest's slave and cut off his right ear. [51]But Jesus answered, "Enough of this!" He touched the man's ear and healed him.

[52]Then Jesus said to the chief priests and the officers of the Temple guard and the elders who had come there to get him: "Did you have to come with swords and clubs, as though I were an outlaw? [53]I was with you in the Temple every day, and you did not try to arrest me. But this hour belongs to you and to the power of darkness."

[54]They arrested Jesus and took him away into the house of the High Priest; and Peter followed far behind. [55]A fire had been lit in the

center of the courtyard, and Peter joined those who were sitting around it. ⁵⁶When one of the servant girls saw him sitting there at the fire, she looked straight at him and said, "This man too was with him!" ⁵⁷But Peter denied it: "Woman, I don't even know him!" ⁵⁸After a while, a man noticed him and said, "You are one of them, too!" But Peter answered, "Man, I am not!" ⁵⁹And about an hour later another man insisted strongly: "There isn't any doubt that this man was with him, because he also is a Galilean!" ⁶⁰But Peter answered, "Man, I don't know what you are talking about!" At once, while he was still speaking, a rooster crowed. ⁶¹The Lord turned around and looked straight at Peter, and Peter remembered the Lord's words, how he had said, "Before the rooster crows today, you will say three times that you do not know me." ⁶²Peter went out and wept bitterly.

⁶³The men who were guarding Jesus made fun of him and beat him. ⁶⁴They blindfolded him and asked him, "Who hit you? Guess!" ⁶⁵And they said many other insulting things to him.

⁶⁶When day came, the elders of the Jews, the chief priests, and the teachers of the Law met together, and Jesus was brought to their Council. ⁶⁷"Tell us," they said, "are you the Messiah?" He answered: "If I tell you, you will not believe me, ⁶⁸and if I ask you a question you will not answer me. ⁶⁹But from now on the Son of Man will be seated at the right side of the Almighty God." ⁷⁰They all said, "Are you, then, the Son of God?" He answered them, "You say that I am." ⁷¹And they said, "We don't need any witnesses! We ourselves have heard his very own words!"

The trial of Jesus before the Roman governor, Pontius Pilate, in 23:1–5 stresses the political nature of the charges brought by the Jewish leaders, and insists that Pilate declared Jesus to be innocent of those political charges. Pilate is represented here as a just governor who saw through the false accusations of the Jewish leaders. Still, perhaps in an effort to avoid a confrontation, he sends Jesus to Herod, the ruler of Galilee.

The trial of Jesus before Herod Antipas in 23:6–16 also affirms Jesus' innocence in the face of these political charges. Again, Jesus keeps silent. The deeds of his accusers indicate who the guilty parties are. Like those persecuted in Luke's time, Jesus exemplifies the true martyr, condemned, though blameless, even in the minds of those who will pass the harsh judgment of death on the cross.

The Sentencing and Death

The story of the sentencing (23:17–25) stresses that Pilate passed the death verdict on Jesus not because he was really guilty, but because the crowd, incited by the chief priests, put pressure on the governor. Jesus' innocence is emphasized in 23:22 ("I cannot find anything he has done to deserve death") and responsibility for Jesus' execution falls on the Jewish leaders.

Jesus Before Pilate
(Also Matt. 27.1–2, 11–14; Mark 15.1–5; John 18.28–38)

23 The whole group rose up and took Jesus before Pilate, ²where they began to accuse him: "We caught this man misleading our people, telling them not to pay taxes to the Emperor and claiming that he himself is Christ, a king." ³Pilate asked him, "Are you the king of the Jews?" "You say it," answered Jesus. ⁴Then Pilate said to the chief priests and the crowds, "I find no reason to condemn this man." ⁵But they insisted even more strongly, "He is starting a riot among the people with his teaching! He began in Galilee, went through all of Judea, and now has come here."

⁶When Pilate heard this he asked, "Is this man a Galilean?" ⁷When he learned that Jesus was from the region ruled by Herod, he sent him to Herod, who was also in Jerusalem at that time. ⁸Herod was very pleased when he saw Jesus, for he had heard about him and had been wanting to see him for a long time; he was hoping to see Jesus perform some miracle. ⁹So Herod asked Jesus many questions, but Jesus did not answer a word. ¹⁰The chief priests and the teachers of the Law stepped forward and made strong accusations against Jesus. ¹¹Herod and his soldiers made fun of Jesus and treated him with contempt. They put a fine robe on him and sent him back to Pilate. ¹²On that very day Herod and Pilate became friends; they had been enemies before this.

Jesus Is Sentenced to Death
(Also Matt. 27.15–26; Mark 15.6–15; John 18.39–19.16)

¹³Pilate called together the chief priests, the leaders, and the people, ¹⁴and said to them: "You brought this man to me and said that he was misleading the people. Now, I have examined him here in your presence, and I have not found him guilty of any of the bad things you accuse him of. ¹⁵Nor did Herod find him guilty, for he sent him back to us. There is nothing this man has done to deserve death. ¹⁶I will

have him whipped, then, and let him go." [¹⁷At each Passover Feast Pilate had to set free one prisoner for them.] ¹⁸The whole crowd cried out, "Kill him! Set Barabbas free for us!" (¹⁹Barabbas had been put in prison for a riot that had taken place in the city, and for murder.) ²⁰Pilate wanted to set Jesus free, so he called out to the crowd again. ²¹But they shouted back, "To the cross with him! To the cross!" ²²Pilate said to them the third time: "But what crime has he committed? I cannot find anything he has done to deserve death! I will have him whipped and set him free." ²³But they kept on shouting at the top of their voices that Jesus should be nailed to the cross; and finally their shouting won. ²⁴So Pilate passed the sentence on Jesus that they were asking for. ²⁵He set free the man they wanted, the one who had been put in prison for riot and murder, and turned Jesus over to them to do as they wished.

The crucifixion account (23:33–43) shows that Jesus was faithful to his Father's will and to his own teaching of loving one's enemies, that he withstood bravely the three temptations to prove that he was the Messiah (23:35–43), that he was an innocent sufferer, and that he presisted in his ministry to outsiders to the very end of his earthly life (23:39–43). At this most decisive point in his life, Jesus prays to God as Father. He gives a sign of his being the Messiah, not by giving in to the familiar temptation to show his glory, but by offering forgiveness to the soldiers and to the man crucified with him. Even in death (23:44–49), Jesus is faithful to his Father's will, and his innocence is confirmed by the centurion. The tearing of the Temple curtain symbolized the beginning of the new covenant. No longer would God's people relate to him through the Temple, but directly in Christ.

The story of Jesus' burial (23:50–56) insists that Jesus was really dead and that the women who went to the tomb on Easter Sunday did not go to the wrong place. Joseph himself took the body down from the cross, and the women accompanied him to the tomb. When they returned after the Sabbath to anoint Jesus, there can be no doubt that they came to the right place.

■ Reflection

Are there any principles for which I would be willing to undergo suffering and death?

Jesus Is Nailed to the Cross
(Also Matt. 27.32–44; Mark 15.21–32; John 19.17–27)

²⁶They took Jesus away. As they went, they met a man named Simon, from Cyrene, who was coming into the city from the country. They seized him, put the cross on him and made him carry it behind Jesus.

²⁷A large crowd of people followed him; among them were some women who were weeping and wailing for him. ²⁸Jesus turned to them and said: "Women of Jerusalem! Don't cry for me, but for yourselves and your children. ²⁹For the days are coming when people will say, 'How lucky are the women who never had children, who never bore babies, who never nursed them!' ³⁰That will be the time when people will say to the mountains, 'Fall on us!' and to the hills, 'Hide us!' ³¹For if such things as these are done when the wood is green, what will it be like when it is dry?"

³²They took two others also, both of them criminals, to be put to death with Jesus. ³³When they came to the place called "The Skull," they nailed Jesus to the cross there, and the two criminals, one on his right and one

on his left. ³⁴Jesus said, "Forgive them, Father! They don't know what they are doing." They divided his clothes among themselves by throwing dice. ³⁵The people stood there watching, while the Jewish leaders made fun of him: "He saved others; let him save himself, if he is the Messiah whom God has chosen!" ³⁶The soldiers also made fun of him; they came up to him and offered him wine, ³⁷and said, "Save yourself, if you are the king of the Jews!" ³⁸These words were written above him: "This is the King of the Jews."

³⁹One of the criminals hanging there threw insults at him: "Aren't you the Messiah? Save yourself and us!" ⁴⁰The other one, however, rebuked him, saying: "Don't you fear God? Here we are all under the same sentence. ⁴¹Ours, however, is only right, for we are getting what we deserve for what we did; but he has done no wrong." ⁴²And he said to Jesus, "Remember me, Jesus, when you come as King!" ⁴³Jesus said to him, "I tell you this: today you will be in Paradise with me."

⁴⁴It was about twelve o'clock when the sun stopped shining and darkness covered the whole country until three o'clock; ⁴⁵and the curtain hanging in the Temple was torn in two. ⁴⁶Jesus cried out in a loud voice, "Father! In your hands I place my spirit!" He said this and died. ⁴⁷The army officer saw what had happened, and he praised God, saying, "Certainly he was a good man!" ⁴⁸When the people who had gathered there to watch the spectacle saw what happened, they all went back home beating their breasts. ⁴⁹All those who knew Jesus personally, including the women who had followed him from Galilee, stood off at a distance to see these things.

The Burial of Jesus
(Also Matt. 27.57–61; Mark 15.42–47; John 19.38–42)

[50-51]There was a man named Joseph, from the Jewish town of Arimathea. He was a good and honorable man, and waited for the coming of the Kingdom of God. Although a member of the Council, he had not agreed with their decision and action. [52]He went into the presence of Pilate and asked for the body of Jesus. [53]Then he took the body down, wrapped it in a linen sheet, and placed it in a grave which had been dug out of the rock—a grave which had never been used. [54]It was Friday, and the Sabbath was about to begin.

[55]The women who had followed Jesus from Galilee went with Joseph and saw the grave and how Jesus' body was laid in it. [56]Then they went back home and prepared the spices and ointments for his body.

On the Sabbath they rested, as the Law commanded.

The Empty Tomb

The discovery of the empty tomb (24:1–12) sets the stage for the appearances in the remainder of the chapter. The emptiness of the tomb does not prove the resurrection of Jesus, but any talk about the resurrection would have been senseless if the tomb were not empty. The first witnesses to the empty tomb were women, who in ancient times were not considered qualified witnesses in trials or assemblies. They themselves were taken by surprise, and the other disciples did not take them seriously. Even when Peter verifies their story, he does not connect this event with Jesus' predictions of the resurrection.

The Appearances

The appearance of the risen Jesus to the two disciples on the road to Emmaus (24:13–35) brings together many of the great themes of the Gospel of Luke. It emphasizes the presence of the risen Jesus in the Christian community through the witness of the Old Testament and the community's meals.

The dialogue between Jesus and the two disciples (24:17–27) elicits a description of Jesus' earthly life. The disciples recognize Jesus only when they share a meal with him. The story ends in 24:33–35 when the two disciples report to the eleven apostles what had happened to them and how they came to recognize Jesus in the Scriptures and the breaking of the bread.

The Resurrection
(Also Matt. 28.1–10; Mark 16.1–8; John 20.1–10)

24 Very early on Sunday morning the women went to the grave carrying the spices they had prepared. ²They found the stone rolled away from the entrance to the grave, ³so they went on in; but they did not find the body of the Lord Jesus. ⁴They stood there uncertain about this, when suddenly two men in bright shining clothes stood by them. ⁵Full of fear, the women bowed down to the ground, as the men said to them: "Why are you looking among the dead for one who is alive? ⁶He is not here; he has risen. Remember what he said to you while he was in Galilee: ⁷'The Son of Man must be handed over to sinful men, be nailed to the cross and be raised to life on the third day.' " ⁸Then the women remembered his words, ⁹returned from the grave, and told all these things to the eleven disciples and all the rest. ¹⁰The women were Mary Magdalene,

Joanna, and Mary the mother of James; they and the other women with them told these things to the apostles. ¹¹But the apostles thought that what the women said was nonsense, and did not believe them. ¹²But Peter got up and ran to the grave; he bent down and saw the grave cloths and nothing else. Then he went back home wondering at what had happened.

The Walk to Emmaus
(Also Mark 16.12–13)

¹³On that same day two of them were going to a village named Emmaus, about seven miles from Jerusalem, ¹⁴and they were talking to each other about all the things that had happened. ¹⁵As they talked and discussed, Jesus himself drew near and walked along with them; ¹⁶they saw him, but somehow did not recognize him. ¹⁷Jesus said to them, "What are you talking about, back and forth, as you walk along?" And they stood still, with sad faces. ¹⁸One of them, named Cleopas, asked him, "Are you the only man living in Jerusalem who does not know what has been happening there these last few days?" ¹⁹"What things?" he asked. "The things that happened to Jesus of Nazareth," they answered. "This man was a prophet, and was considered by God and by all the people to be mighty in words and deeds. ²⁰Our chief priests and rulers handed him over to be sentenced to death, and they nailed him to the cross. ²¹And we had hoped that he would be the one who was going to redeem Israel! Besides all that, this is now the third day since it happened. ²²Some of the women of our group surprised us; they went at dawn to the grave, ²³but could not find his body. They came back saying

they had seen a vision of angels who told them that he is alive. ²⁴Some of our group went to the grave and found it exactly as the women had said, but they did not see him." ²⁵Then Jesus said to them: "How foolish you are, how slow you are to believe everything the prophets said! ²⁶Was it not necessary for the Messiah to suffer these things and enter his glory? ²⁷And Jesus explained to them what was said about him in all the Scriptures, beginning with the books of Moses and the writings of all the prophets.

²⁸They came near the village to which they were going, and Jesus acted as if he were going farther; ²⁹but they held him back, saying, "Stay with us; the day is almost over and it is getting dark." So he went in to stay with them. ³⁰He sat at table with them, took the bread, and said the blessing; then he broke the bread and gave it to them. ³¹Their eyes were opened and they recognized him; but he disappeared from their sight. ³²They said to each other, "Wasn't it like a fire burning in us when he talked to us on the road and explained the Scriptures to us?"

³³They got up at once and went back to Jerusalem, where they found the eleven disciples gathered together with the others ³⁴and saying, "The Lord is risen indeed! Simon has seen him!" ³⁵The two then explained to them what had happened on the road, and how they had recognized the Lord when he broke the bread.

The appearance of the risen Lord to the disciples in Jerusalem (24:36–49) consists of the appearance proper (24:36–46) and the commission (24:47–49). This appearance continues the theme of the communal meal as the place where the risen Lord can be encountered, and reinforces the image of the messianic banquet.

The commission of the disciples echoes some other important Lukan themes. The good news is to be preached to all nations, beginning in Jerusalem. The disciples are witnesses to the fulfillment of the Old Testament in Jesus' life and deeds. They are to preach the Gospel of repentance and the forgiveness of sin.

Jesus promises them the Holy Spirit, the principle of continuity between the time of Jesus and the time of the Church. The Gospel ends with Jesus' blessing and departure in 24:50–53. The story of the ascension is told in detail in Acts 1:9–12.

■ *Reflection*

Who is the Jesus we recognize in the breaking of the bread at Mass?

Jesus Appears to His Disciples
(Also Matt. 28.16–20; Mark 16.14–18; John 20.19–23; Acts 1.6–8)

³⁶While they were telling them this, suddenly the Lord himself stood among them and said to them, "Peace be with you." ³⁷Full of fear and terror, they thought that they were seeing a ghost. ³⁸But he said to them: "Why are you troubled? Why are these doubts coming up in your minds? ³⁹Look at my hands and my feet and see that it is I, myself. Feel me, and you will see, for a ghost doesn't have flesh and bones, as you can see I have." ⁴⁰He said this and showed them his hands and his feet. ⁴¹They still could not believe, they were so full of joy and wonder; so he asked them, "Do you have anything to eat here?" ⁴²They gave him a piece of cooked fish, ⁴³which he took and ate before them.

⁴⁴Then he said to them: "These are the very things I told while I was still with you: every-

thing written about me in the Law of Moses, the writings of the prophets, and the Psalms had to come true." ⁴⁵Then he opened their minds to understand the Scriptures, ⁴⁶and said to them: "This is what is written: that the Messiah must suffer and be raised from death on the third day, ⁴⁷and that in his name the message about repentance and the forgiveness of sins must be preached to all nations, beginning with Jerusalem. ⁴⁸You are witnesses of these things. ⁴⁹And I myself will send upon you what my Father has promised. But you must wait in the city until the power from above comes down upon you."

⁵⁰Then he led them out of the city as far as Bethany, where he raised his hands and blessed them. ⁵¹As he was blessing them, he departed from them and was taken up into heaven. ⁵²They worshiped him and went back into Jerusalem, filled with great joy, ⁵³and spent all their time in the Temple giving thanks to God.

■ Discussion

1. How does Luke bring out Jesus' innocence?

2. How do the concluding chapters of the Gospel add to Luke's portrait of Jesus as a prophet. a martyr, and an example?

3. How do the appearances in chapter 24 summarize the major themes of the Gospel?

4. What parallels can you find between the story of the journey to Emmaus and the celebration of the Eucharist?

5. What role has the Holy Spirit played throughout the Gospel of Luke?

■ Prayer and Meditation

"The LORD says,
'Here is my servant whom I strengthen—
    the one I have chosen, with whom I am pleased.
I have filled him with my spirit,
    and he will bring justice to every nation.
He will not shout or raise his voice
    or make loud speeches in the streets.
He will not break off a bent reed
    nor put out a flickering lamp.
He will bring lasting justice to all.
He will not lose hope or courage;
    he will establish justice on the earth.
Distant lands eagerly wait for his teaching.' "

Isaiah 42:1–4

Bibliography

GENERAL
J.A. Fitzmyer, *The Gospel According to Luke (I–IX).* Garden City, NY: Doubleday, 1981.

E. LaVerdiere, *Luke.* Wilmington, DE: Michael Glazier, Inc., 1980.

I.H. Marshall, *The Gospel of Luke. A Commentary on the Greek Text.* Grand Rapids, MI: Eerdmans, 1978.

STUDY SESSION ONE
R.E. Brown, *An Adult Christ at Christmas.* Collegeville, MN: Liturgical Press, 1978.

————, *The Birth of the Messiah.* Garden City, NY: Doubleday, 1977.

STUDY SESSION TWO
P.S. Minear, *To Heal and to Reveal. The Prophetic Vocation According to Luke.* New York, NY: Seabury, 1976.

D.L. Tiede, *Prophecy and History in Luke-Acts.* Philadelphia, PA: Fortress Press, 1980.

STUDY SESSION THREE
J. Piper, *"Love Your Enemies." Jesus' Love Command.* New York, NY–London: Cambridge University Press, 1979.

A. Weiser, *The Miracles of Jesus Then and Now.* Chicago, IL: Franciscan Herald, 1972.

STUDY SESSION FOUR

D. Gill, "Observations on the Lukan Travel Narrative and Some Related Passages," *Harvard Theological Review* 63, (1970), 199–221.

J. Navone, *Themes of St. Luke.* Rome: Gregorian Press, 1971.

STUDY SESSION FIVE

R.J. Cassidy, *Jesus, Politics, and Society. A Study of Luke's Gospel.* Maryknoll, NY: Orbis, 1978.

L.T. Johnson. *The Literary Functions of Possessions in Luke-Acts.* Chico, CA: Scholars, 1977.

D.L. Mealand, *Poverty and Expectation in the Gospels.* London: SPCK, 1980.

STUDY SESSION SIX

R.J. Dillon, *From Eye-Witnesses to Ministers of the Word.* Rome: Biblical Institute Press, 1978.

N. Perrin, *The Resurrection According to Matthew, Mark, and Luke.* Philadelphia, PA: Fortress Press, 1977.

D.M. Stanley, *Jesus in Gethsemane.* New York, NY — Ramsey, NJ — Toronto: Paulist, 1980.

P.W. Walasky, "The Trial and Death of Jesus in the Gospel of Luke," *Journal of Biblical Literature* 94, (1975), 81–93.